DIVIDE AND CONQUER
2,731 Miles Out Living It on Two Wheels

Self-Published By:
Brent Goldstein

All rights reserved. No part of this book may be reproduced or transmitted in any form or by any means, electronic or mechanical, including photocopying, recording or by an information storage and retrieval system – except by a reviewer who may quote brief passages in a review to be printed in a magazine or newspaper – without permission in writing from the author.

Copyright © 2019 by Brent Goldstein
Printed in the United States of America
Second Edition

ISBN: 978-0-9600517-1-7

Cover Photo Credit: Vincent Hamel
Book Cover Design: Kristine Go

"To Change Lives To Live With Passion To Out Live It"

— *Out Living It Project*
www.firstdescents.org

PROLOGUE – "Well I've got such a long way to go,
To make it to the border of Mexico,
So I'll ride like the wind, ride like the wind."
— Christopher Cross, *Ride Like The Wind*

"FUCK!!!" A nasty concoction of hunger, dehydration, exhaustion, oxygen-deprivation and shivering cold reduced my thoughts to one four-letter word. My (somewhat) sincere apologies to those under 15 years old or those easily offended by colorful language. I languished on a slick and muddy dirt logging road 50 miles from the nearest civilization, the ski resort town of Fernie, British Columbia, Canada. It was only 11:30AM and I had already been riding my mountain bike for five hours. Actually, wishful thinking best describes the term "riding" as three of those hours included the most pernicious section of steep craggy hike-a-bike evil that I had ever experienced. Worst of all, at that expletive-filled moment, a peanut-buttery mud caked my tires, my drive train, my pedals and my chain, restraining all forward movement. After clearing the mud from the frame and tires with my numb fingers for the fifth time, I slammed the bike into the weeds on the side of the road in disgust and exasperation.

Laugh, cry or pass out. Those were my options. I was miserable. I was despondent. I was scared. I was borderline delirious. Most of all, my mental weakness pissed me off. Why was I unable to do what I taught my kids to do since birth in tough situations and SUCK IT UP? Where was the flip to switch? I knew the Tour Divide would be hard and uncomfortable, but I did not bargain for abject misery. FUUUUUUCK!

I eventually alit in Fernie, checked into the first hotel on the left, and heaved my bike into the back corner of a large storage closet. I then ambled dejectedly to my room, tossed all of my disgusting clothes into the bathtub, called Lisa (my wife) and begged her to find me the next shuttle to the nearest airport. Two days in and I was DONE. The hardest bike race in the world claimed an early victim.

Chapter 1 – "And you may ask yourself,
 "Well... how did I get here?"
 — Talking Heads, *Once in a Lifetime*

Allan ("Al") Goldberg and I were born seven weeks apart at George Washington Hospital in Washington D.C. in the summer of 1967. However, we did not meet until the summer of 1974 at the Bar-T-Ranch day camp in the D.C. suburbs. I remember the specific moment. While messing around in the swimming pool, I spied a kid (Al) sitting in a tattered folding chair, clad in denim overalls and looking bored. From the edge of the pool, I asked, "Hey there, why aren't you swimming and why are you dressed like a farmer?" He shot me a look of disdain and did not respond. I returned to a game of Marco Polo.

Al and I met again a few months later in Ms. Vennedrow's second grade class at Cold Spring Elementary in Potomac, Maryland. As Goldberg and Goldstein, our seats were adjacent. Through such close proximity, we bonded over a shared passion for local sports. At least five times that fall, Ms. Vennedrow summoned both of us to her desk and implored us to save our "Warner Wolf moments" for recess (Warner Wolf was a famous local sportscaster at the time). We liked Ms. Vennedrow because she knew of Warner Wolf. Regardless, she finally gave up in frustration and separated us.

Despite Ms. Vennedrow's classroom relocation, Al and I became best friends. We were inseparable from elementary school through high school. I attended my first rock concerts (AC/DC and Rush) with Al, drank my first beer with Al, and co-starred in hundreds of juvenile escapades with Al. With so much time spent at each other's houses, we practically shared parents, dogs and siblings. We attended colleges that were an hour apart (Syracuse and Colgate), and many memorable college weekends began with a phone call from Al starting with something like, "Hey BG, get your ass up to the 'Cuse Saturday evening. Big mixer at the house. Don't ask any questions, just be here."

Our lives diverged after college as Al went to the west coast and points beyond to sow his wild oats, while I returned to Washington to toil through law school, get married (Al was a groomsman, of course), reproduce, and do the conventional career thing. However, we always stayed in close communication and saw each other several times a year via ski trips, Vegas trips, weddings, beach trips, reunions and Al's frequent visits home.

Al was a special friend ... my prototypical "brother from another mother" ... but he was also a special human being. At age 12, Al suffered a vicious and rare form of cancer known as Rhabdomyosarcoma. Despite enduring massive blasts of chemotherapy and radiation, and despite survival odds of less than five percent, Al miraculously lived. This experience shaped his personality, as he believed that overcoming those odds empowered him with indomitability and the means to accomplish anything. He resembled the John Locke character in the TV show *Lost* whose mantra was, "Don't tell me what I can't do!" That was vintage Al. If he wanted to do something, it got done. To illustrate, on one of my visits to Syracuse, Al and I casually shared beers at a bar called Fagan's when Al matter-of-factly proclaimed, "I'd like to be a bouncer at this bar."

I looked at him with a sardonic smile and responded, "Dude, you are five foot six and 140 pounds. Maybe they'll hire you as a busboy!"

A week later, he hit the gym with fury and passion and, within six months, he transformed himself from a skinny kid into a mini Adonis. Al got the bouncer job and held it through college graduation.

Moving on from his 'sculpted' phase, Al became a marathon runner in his 20s and ultimately an Ironman triathlete. For those not familiar with an Ironman triathlon, it is a one-day event where an athlete swims 2.4 miles, bikes 112 miles and THEN runs a full marathon. Only truly elite athletes or really really stubborn people are capable of completing these events. Al was both.

On a higher plane, Al not only continued to spit in the face of childhood cancer by testing his physical limits, but he also felt a deep obligation to draw from his personal cancer experience to "pay it forward" to others fighting the sinister disease. This started with volunteer work and later a full-time position with the Okizu foundation in California, an organization that operates peer support programs for children and families affected by childhood cancer. But that was not enough. Al had loftier plans to satisfy his calling. In 2004, the Kennedy School at Harvard University accepted Al into its Public Administration graduate program where he earned a Masters Degree. With a Harvard degree in hand, Al was eager to change the world.

Following Harvard, Al took a job with the Lance Armstrong Foundation (LAF) in Austin, Texas. Those were the days when Lance was still a demi-god and LAF was the gold standard in philanthropy. While Al loved his work with LAF, an amazing opportunity arose in the spring of 2006 when Brad Ludden, professional kayaker and founder of the fledgling First Descents cancer organization in Vail, Colorado, asked Al to take command as Executive Director. First Descents' mission is to run outdoor adventure programs for young adults coping with cancer.

Al and I met over beers and discussed the pros and cons of departing LAF for First Descents. Leaving one of the most recognized philanthropic organizations in the world for an unknown outfit made Al nervous. However, I pointed out that First Descents sounded like a perfect fit as he could take over a grassroots organization, shape it in his image, grow it and, most importantly, pursue a mission that combined his passions – the outdoors, fighting cancer and overcoming physical odds. I added, "Plus, you'll get to live in Vail, Colorado for your job! How sweet is that?"

Al responded, "Yeah, pretty sweet, brother. Pretty sweet."

He took the job.

In August 2006, just weeks after moving to Vail and days after starting his new job, Al experienced unusual back pains. He initially shrugged off the soreness as a typical ailment of an athlete, but the pain persisted and worsened. Amid growing concern, Al visited a doctor who performed a number of tests that confirmed his worst fears. Cancer had unceremoniously returned after a 27-year hiatus.

Al shared the news with me over the phone. He surprisingly sounded upbeat and dismissive. I asked what I could do for him and here is how the conversation went:

Al: "Yes, there is something you can do for me. You can get off the damn couch and do an Ironman triathlon with me next summer."
Me: "That's hilarious Al, but I do NOT run and will only get in a pool if you give me a raft and a beer or three!
Al: "Yeah, I knew you were going to say that, so I have something else more your speed."
Me: "Oh shit, here it comes."
Al: "You are still mountain-biking right?"
Me: "Uh, yeah."
Al: "Great, do some training. We're racing the Leadville 100 mountain bike race together next August."

The Leadville 100 is an iconic one-day 100+ mile mountain bike race based in Leadville, Colorado. It starts at an altitude of 10,200 feet, climbs as high as 12,600 feet, and consists of cumulative elevation gains of over 13,000 feet. To be an official finisher, one must complete the race in under 12 hours. This was more my speed only because it involved riding a mountain bike in a forward direction, but that was hardly a qualification considering I had never in my life ridden a bike more than 15 miles at once.

Before I even formulated the word "no," Al continued, "I don't want to hear no. I have to suffer through six months of chemo and radiation, so you

can fucking do this!"
   Me: "Really Al? You are going to play the cancer card already?"
   Al: "Too soon?"
   Me: "You asshole!"
   I accèpted the challenge, hired a coach and trained my ass off for eight months. During this time, Al likewise trained . . . while also enduring chemo and radiation treatments.
   On August 11, 2007, a month shy of my 40th birthday, Al and I lined up at the start of the Leadville 100. Al made it 40 grueling miles, but missed the first mid-race cut-off time by several minutes. Between the chemo treatments, Al's busy schedule with his new job and his generally novice mountain biking skills, I was amazed he made it as far as he did. Talk about iron will. Forced from the bike, he seamlessly transitioned from racer to the best damn crewman/cheerleader in Leadville. Knute Rockne would have swelled with pride from Al's pep talk at mile 60, all while simultaneously massaging a growing cramp in my calf.
   Despite dehydration, stomach issues and massive thigh, quad and calf cramps, I finished the race in 11 hours and 11 minutes, earning a coveted silver buckle (awarded to those who finish in less than 12 hours). When I crossed the finish line, Al tackled me with a huge bear hug and practically burned my skin from his radiating beams of gratification and joy. I am 100% certain that he felt more excitement from my accomplishment than if he had achieved it himself. Of course in classic Al fashion, he looked me in the eye and announced on the spot, "I don't know what you are doing next year, but I'll be back to slay this beast!"
   I looked at him just as squarely in the eye and told him, "I am happy to come back and crew for you, but there is NO FRICKIN' WAY I will ever put myself through that hell again."
The next morning after the race, I called Al and said, "OK asshole, I'm coming back next year . . . only faster!"

Brent and Al - 1974

Al and Brent - 2007

Chapter 2 – "If I had the world to give, I'd give it to you . . ."
— Grateful Dead, *If I had the World to Give*

Al's challenge to race the Leadville 100, and my successful completion of the race in 2007, are only half the story. . . . and the least important half. As previously mentioned, just prior to his cancer re-diagnosis in August 2006, Allan moved to Vail, Colorado to take the Executive Director job with First Descents. When Al took over, First Descents offered five weeklong kayak programs in Montana and Colorado and collected annual revenues (i.e. donations) of less than $300,000. Al and founder Brad Ludden had grandiose goals for First Descents. They dreamed of dramatic financial growth, expansive programming beyond kayaking, and eventual recognition as a national and possibly international organization.

After accepting Al's challenge to race the 2007 Leadville 100, I quickly realized that training for Leadville was going to utilize hundreds of hours of precious time. This required major time-management for me, and significant sacrifice for my family. From a flash of inspiration mixed with a modicum of justification (and a dose of guilt-appeasement), an idea germinated. Maybe we could construct a platform around the Leadville 100 to raise money for First Descents. Al loved the idea. However, we faced a big hurdle as coveted spots in Leadville were only awarded through a lottery held in January. Disheartingly, the ratio of lottery entrants to lottery winners was over 5 to 1.

I am a planner and have minimal patience. Waiting until January to know whether we were racing was not an option. Since the "cancer card" worked on me, I suggested to Al that it might similarly sway the Leadville race organizers. Al said, "I've got this," and in September 2006 he drove to Leadville to meet and share our story with the Leadville 100 race directors and founders, Ken Chlouber and Merilee Maupin.

Al's charm and persuasion obviously struck paydirt. He called me following the meeting and said, "I've got some good news and bad news. The good news is that we have been given 6 lottery-waived spots in the 2007 race."

"That's awesome," I answered, "but what is the bad news?"

With a slight cackle, Al responded, "The bad news, my friend, is that now you have to do the damn race with me!"

With the other spots, I convinced four mountain biking buddies (Gary Morris, Kevin Kane, Dean Gregory and John Wontrobski) to join us in Leadville and we became "Team First Descents" or "Team FD" for short.

During the winter and spring, Al and I spent numerous hours on the phone discussing the race, training, logistics and our fundraising campaign. In May of 2007, Al and I crafted a perfectly-worded donation solicitation email which I sent to my entire Contacts list. A tale that combined friendship, cancer and an iconic race obviously struck a chord as we successfully raised nearly $90,000 for First Descents by the time I crossed the finish line in Leadville. One week after the race, First Descents honored me with an invitation to join its Board of Directors.

The fall, winter and spring of 2007-2008 were bittersweet. Joining the First Descents' board and sharing the endeavor with my best friend were rewarding. During that nine-month period, I spent more time talking with Al than during the prior ten years combined. Unfortunately, this period sadly marked a noticeable decline in Al's health.

Month after month, Al continually reassured me that his weakening was "nothing more than the effects of the post-cancer treatments," and that he would be back to his old self by summer. He was the toughest guy I knew, so I took his word for it. His common refrain when I questioned his appearance was, "Who you 'gonna believe, me or your lyin' eyes?"

By spring of 2008, it was clear from his gaunt and sallow appearance that he was either deluding everyone else or deluding himself.

In late May 2008, Al fainted and an ambulance rushed him to the hospital. Following the frightening episode, he again assured all of us — me, his sisters, parents and other close friends — that this was nothing more than an "enzyme imbalance caused by some lingering cancer cells," and that there was "this great new medication" that would get him back to normal once and for all.

Right after Memorial Day weekend, I gave Al a quick call to check in.

"It's all good here," Al told me. "I'm starting a new medication protocol at the end of the week and then heading to the Outer Banks in North Carolina to spend a week with the family."

"Are you sure you are strong enough to travel?" I inquired with concern.

"I'll be fine," he assured me. "I just need some time to relax and then I'll be back on track! Big summer ahead, bruthah! Lots of riding, getting me over the Leadville hump and you raising beaucoup bucks for FD again!"

What he did not say was that this "medication protocol" was a full-blown chemotherapy treatment and that his condition was quite dire.

Somehow, Al took a 2-hour shuttle straight from chemotherapy in Vail to the airport in Denver, boarded a cross-country flight, and made it to the Outer Banks. I say somehow because I later learned from a nurse at the Shaw Cancer Center in Vail that Al was so weak, sick and frail following the chemotherapy that he could barely stand.

Allan Goldberg, my lifelong buddy, died on Sunday morning, June 22, 2008. The lightning-fast physical deterioration that his body suffered in those last weeks of his life is too painful to recount. Gratifyingly, Al's final days were meaningful and rewarding. He spent time with his family at the beach, one of his favorite places, and then returned to his boyhood home in Potomac, Maryland where he spent part of the last day of his life with two of his oldest friends, Brian Katz and me. Together, we told stories and then watched a Washington Redskins 1982 Super Bowl highlight DVD. This brought back great memories for all three of us of one of the most joyous experiences of our teenage years.

Although his last official breath was at a hospital on that fateful Sunday morning, Al never spent a night in the hospital and gracefully avoided withering away with tubes in his arms and heavy doses of sedative medications. For that, we were all grateful.

Al flabbergasted all of his close friends and family by masterfully hiding his condition from all of us. Al gave his doctors strict orders not to disclose any details of his health during his lifetime. Following his passing, however, we learned from Al's doctors that his prognosis in the summer of 2006 was very poor and that Al astonished all of his caregivers by living another two years. They did not foresee his lasting a year.

Apparently, the cancer had spread throughout his body at least a year before his death. Even in the face of such reality, which he either flatly denied or simply ignored, Al tirelessly fulfilled his professional duties with First Descents. In addition to overseeing almost 100% growth in programming from 2007 to 2008, Al spent nearly all of March 2008 traveling around the United States raising money and establishing strategic partnerships with hospitals and complementary organizations, all while physically deteriorating. Forget the physical strength required. What astonishes me is the amount of mental strength, courage and fortitude he possessed and projected. Al abhorred sympathy and he never EVER used cancer as an excuse for anything. He always fulfilled commitments and kept promises . . . even afternoon meetings fresh off invasive morning treatments. "Inspiration" and "hero" are words I will always associate with Al.

"Complete mess" is the term that best described me in the days and weeks after Al's passing. No instruction manuals aptly prescribe how to deal with the death of your oldest and best friend. Sitting and wallowing were not options, as that would have pissed Al off. I felt numb. I needed redirection. Without any better ideas, I focused on my bike training for Leadville and applied my extra energy into another huge fundraiser for

First Descents in Al's memory.

On a long training ride a few days after the funeral, I starkly realized that I knew very little about First Descents. Yes, I served on the Board and yes, I spent countless hours with Al strategizing over growth plans, revenue projections and other metrics. However, I had never volunteered at a program, had never interacted with any program participants, and did not yet understand the "special sauce" that made a First Descents' experience so special and life changing. In short, Al bridged my involvement with First Descents and fed my passion for fundraising. Without Al, I needed a substantive purpose to back First Descents with the same vigor as the prior year.

Ironically, a couple months before his passing, Al convinced my wife to join him as a volunteer at a First Descents' kayak program in Montana scheduled for the second week of July 2008. Al's death threw a monkey-wrench into those plans, as Lisa felt too upset to attend without him and wanted to cancel her trip. I understood her feelings, but convinced her of three things. First, she needed to live up to her commitment, as her absence would leave the program short-staffed. Second, she would disappoint Al if she cancelled. Third and most importantly, this might be her only chance to experience First Descents first hand. To continue our support, we needed her personal participation and affirmation. Lisa reluctantly agreed and, with emotions boiling over, flew to Montana and attended the program.

While in Montana, Lisa wrote and forwarded to me an emotional and descriptive daily blog. For seven days, I lived and felt the experience through her poignant and powerful words. That week's impact on Lisa changed our lives forever. Lisa became a volunteer *emeritus* and my path as a supporter and board member set in cement.

A month after Lisa's program, I raced the Leadville 100 with fierce passion and profound emotion. My pain was still deep and raw, and the bike race and First Descents were conduits that kept me emotionally connected to Allan's life after death and helped soothe and expedite the mourning process. Rewardingly, our team of riders raised over $120,000 for First Descents.

A year later, my fellow members of the First Descents' Board elected me as their Chairman and I have yet to relinquish the title. Every August I continue to line-up at the Leadville 100 starting line and, to date, the Leadville fundraiser has raised nearly $1.5 Million for First Descents. Most pertinently, I have volunteered at multiple weeklong First Descents' programs and each one reaffirms my commitment to the organization and bolsters my conviction that our mission is important, impactful and even magical.

Brad Ludden and Allan Goldberg's visions for First Descents are now closer to realization. First Descents currently offers 100 programs annually in locations all over the United States and internationally, and its offerings have expanded to include multiple outdoor sports such as surfing, rock-climbing, trekking and ice climbing. Since 2007, First Descents' annual budget has grown from $300,000 to $4,000,000. My small contribution to this growth as a fundraiser and Board Member is the most worthwhile and impactful thing I will do in my life and, other than my children, is the source of my greatest pride. First Descents' success is also the best legacy imaginable to keep Allan Goldberg's memory alive.

Chapter 3 – "This is my quest, to follow that star,
no matter how hopeless, no matter how far,
to fight for the right, without question or pause,
to be willing to march into hell,
for a heavenly cause"
— Andy Williams, *The Impossible Dream*

Following Al's passing, biking and mountain bike racing became central themes in my life, with the Leadville 100 always the shiniest beacon levitating over my annual horizon. In August 2016, I completed my 10th Leadville 100. Ten years passed in the blink of an eye, but they represent a significant chunk of my adult life. During that time, I metamorphosed from a 175-pound doughboy to a respectable 158-pound middle-aged athlete. While I may never compete with elite bike racers, I became a strong recreational rider and constantly scouted new challenges to supplement my annual Leadville fix. It was one of those challenges, one that resided deep and dormant in my subconscious, that was unleashed in the summer of 2017.

Early in my nascent bike racing career, my friend and Leadville cohort Gary Morris dragged me and several other biking buddies to a one-night-only showing of an independent film called "Ride the Divide." The movie was a documentary depicting a new and relatively unknown underground mountain bike race called the "Tour Divide." The Tour Divide consisted of 2,700+ off-road miles down the Continental Divide on a prescribed route starting in Banff, Alberta, Canada and ending at the US/Mexico border in Antelope Wells, New Mexico. What makes the race unique is that there are no aid stations, support vehicles, support crew or specified stopping points. The clock starts every year at the Banff YWCA at 8AM on the second Friday in June and runs continuously until a racer reaches the Mexico border. Whatever racers need to survive (food, water, shelter, clothes, tools, etc.), they have to carry or buy on their own and any unauthorized route deviations result in disqualification. The movie centered on the 2009 Tour Divide, when 16 racers participated and less than half of them finished.

I watched the film in a state of entrancement. Though I rightfully determined that everyone choosing to compete in this race was certifiably nuts, the movie sparked some figurative kindling in the tucked-away part of my brain that harbored youthful dreams and fantasies of adventure beyond simply racing in Leadville every summer.

Over the ensuing years, the Tour Divide's visibility increased in mountain bike culture as the race burgeoned from that 16 riders to over

170 riders by 2016. While those kindled embers in my brain still awaited stoking, a friend from my bike universe, Bonnie Gagnon, participated in and completed the Tour Divide in 2016. To exhaust the fire metaphor, knowing someone who finished the race served as the flint to start a cerebral campfire, and the race formally elevated itself from murky dream status to bucket-list status. Regardless, I still viewed the race as so crazy and so ridiculous that I dared not share the momentous status change with anyone, including Lisa.

Fast forward to early summer 2017. Lisa and I were driving across the country when the topic of Leadville came up. In less than two months, I would compete in my 11th consecutive Leadville 100. Lisa asked me if I had any time goals and I responded negatively. Sensing that I did not seem to have my usual excitement for the race, she asked, "Honey, are you bored with Leadville?"

I silently stared out the windshield and pondered this question for a few minutes. Leadville had defined much of my self-identity over the past ten years, specifically as a graying athlete. While I had added dozens of races and centuries (i.e. 100-miles on a bike) and interval workouts and hill-repeats to my repertoire over the years, Leadville was always the ultimate annual test by which I measured my fitness, toughness, perseverance and desire. I thus surprised myself when the words that escaped my mouth were, "Yes, I am a little bored with Leadville."

Boom!

A few moments of silence ensued, eventually broken by Lisa saying, "Well, I know you and I am pretty sure you have some bucket-list goal to either replace or add to Leadville. Come clean. What is it?"

Once again, I reflected for a minute. She actually used the term "bucket-list." Hmmm. Do I really want to say what I am about to say? Will she be dismissive? Angry? Surprised? Will she grab the steering wheel and head straight for the nearest mental facility . . . or divorce lawyer? Well, here goes nothing. I asked, "Have you ever heard of a bike race called the Tour Divide?" She shook her head no, and I proceeded to tell her about the "Ride the Divide" documentary and the race itself.

Noticing my increased animation, Lisa asked with trepidation whether the race was something that I would ever consider. To put her mind at ease, I assured her that it was not yet on my radar screen, but maybe I would take a harder look when the kids are out of college and I have more free time.

After a few long moments, Lisa turned to me and asked with a whiff of derision, "The fact that you are even considering something like this reeks of mid-life crisis. Is that what this is?"

I glanced at her and said, "I dunno. Maybe. Could be. Who the hell knows?"

We drove on for a few miles without saying a word. I sensed the Lisa was deeply contemplating something. Breaking the silence, she continued, "Well, you ARE turning 50 in a few months."

"Yeah, so what?"

Then, nearly 11 years after my fateful phone call with Al, my world careened off its axis once again when Lisa responded with, "So, you aren't getting any younger. Why wait until the kids are gone? You should do it next summer."

Me, spontaneously combusting, said, "Wait . . . WHAT?!?!? You think this is a good idea and you think I should do it NEXT SUMMER?"

"No," she responded with a slight edge to her voice, "it is far and away the most idiotic asinine stupid idea I have ever heard, but if you are going to do it, do it now. Who knows what the future holds?"

Still shaking my head in disbelief, I added, "You realize that I will be gone for four to five weeks?" Before she could even answer, I quickly asked with a chuckle, "Hey, wait a minute. That was too easy! Who's the boyfriend?"

I laughed. She laughed. I married her because she gets my lame humor. Maybe she married me because she knew I would not buy a boat or trade her in for a younger woman when I turned 50!

And that was that. No further discussion.

Unprepared for her response, I drove on in a state of shock. I had not for a second contemplated taking on this challenge so soon. However, this was no time for indecision. I had just won Willie Wonka's golden ticket with the blessing of my beautiful though clearly misguided wife. I was going to commit to race the 2018 Tour Divide.

I immediately started thinking of the fundraising possibilities for First Descents. I was confident that nobody in my community had ever done anything remotely as ambitious and/or crazy as the Tour Divide or even knew anyone who had ever done something similar. In fact, I think 99.9% of all people in my orbit had never even heard of the Tour Divide. This would be a unique story and thus an opportunity to set an aggressive financial goal. The only question was how big would I go?

Donations generated from my Team FD Leadville fundraiser (now promoted under the moniker "Out Living It") produced consistent annual revenues of between $70,000 and $80,000. I hoped that the magnitude and insanity of the Tour Divide would inspire increased largesse. Within days after completing the 2017 Leadville 100, I turned my focus squarely on the 2018 Tour Divide and set an initial fundraising goal in my head of $150,000. By September, the wheels were fully in motion (no pun intended). I just needed a few things such as a touring bike, a tent, bikepacking bags, sleeping bag, sleeping pad, bike computer, headlamps, hydration system, portable power source, plane tickets, a pre-frontal lobotomy and, most importantly, a clue.

Chapter 4 – "I'll always be a dreaming man,
I don't have to understand,
I know it's alright."
— Neil Young, *Dreamin' Man*

    Once I decided to commit to race the Tour Divide, I became an information sponge. First, I typed "Tour Divide" in the *Google* search bar. In 0.40 seconds, *Google* magically revealed multiple pages of links to websites, articles, YouTube videos and books about the race. I spent September and October of 2017 devouring these resources. Then I joined three different Facebook group pages dedicated to the Tour Divide, specifically, and bikepacking, generally. My initial research culminated with an hour-long phone call with my friend and Tour Divide veteran, Bonnie Gagnon from Minnesota. Bonnie patiently answered 127 different questions and offered enough advice about logistics and gear to fill seven pages of single-spaced handwritten notes. As the call wound to its conclusion, I finally asked Bonnie the central question, "How the hell do I formally sign up for this race?"

    Bonnie laughed and said, "Brent, there is no formal application, registration or entry fee for the Tour Divide. Simply send Matthew an email after Thanksgiving stating a desire to race the Tour. And throw in some personal background as well."

    Matthew would be Matthew Lee, the founder of the Tour Divide, a six-time winner of the Tour Divide, and the current "race director" (for lack of a better designation) of the Tour Divide.

    My Thanksgiving turkey was still digesting when I sent Matthew the following email:

> **Dear Matthew:**
> **This email serves as my Letter of Intent to join the other riders/racers/miscreants/idiots as a participant in the 2018 Tour Divide. I plan to go north-south as part of the mass-start from Banff on June 8. This should be particularly interesting as I have not slept in a tent in 35 years and have never bikepacked a day in my life . . . yet. However, I am foolish, I am stubborn, I have a high pain-tolerance, I love to ride, I like being alone, I am suffering from acute mid-life crisis having just turned 50 and I have no time-constraints. The only thing I have to hang my hat on in the biking community is that I am an 11-time Leadville 100 finisher. So now I just need to figure out**

how to ride the Leadville 100 on a 50-pound bike every day for 20-30 consecutive days while starving myself and eluding bears, mountain-lions, mosquitos, rattlesnakes and rabid dogs. Piece of frickin' cake!
Let me know if you need anything else from me.
Thanks, Brent Goldstein

Within ten minutes, Matthew responded as follows:

Awesome Brent. I know you can do it. If you're from Maryland, and you mountain bike, you gotta be tough! (I'm an Appalachian rider, too, so I would know). Work out the little tweaks (mastery of saddle sores), and kit packing / carriage mastery, and you'll be ready.
More info as we enter the spring.
Cheers, Matthew

Holy shit! Apparently, I was officially committed.

Next I created a detailed spreadsheet listing all needed gear, starting with the bike and bike-related accessories, and continuing with electronics, clothing, sleep system, bike bags, lights, hydration options and miscellaneous items such as bug spray, water purification formula, mosquito head-net and bear spray. Once I completed the spreadsheet, the meticulous research began. One to two hours were devoted to each gear item reading backpacking.com, bikepacking.com and Amazon. com reviews before entering the brand name and cost next to the item in the spreadsheet. The process was both painstaking and exciting. I surprisingly discovered a staggering number of opinions regarding the efficacy of sleeping bags versus sleeping quilts, and tents versus bivouac-sacs. Who knew that inflatable sleeping pads had insulation ratings or that tents now came with integrated LED light strands charged via USB?

For my 50th birthday, a group of friends pitched in and bought me a $750 gift-card to REI. I also assisted a friend with a large business transaction. In appreciation, he likewise sent me a sizable REI gift-card. The two gift-cards accounted for 80% of the items on my spreadsheet (#winning!).

Bike selection maximized my research time. Did I want a rigid frame, hard-tail frame or full-suspension frame? What sized tires? What kind of handlebars, grips or pedals? Should I attach multi-colored Ride-Along-Dolly-Streamers to my grips? Should I put playing cards in my tire spokes so that they make that cool "tat-tat-tat-tat" sound that we all loved as kids?

By mid-December, I made my choice — a rigid frame Salsa Fargo — a star among Tour Divide veterans. Unfortunately, in a painful twist of fate just hours before ordering the bike, I bent over to tie my shoes and massively threw out my back. I spent three late December days unable to move from the exact spot where I first crumpled on my bedroom floor, and another two weeks in severe pain with limited mobility. The bike purchase and, more significantly, the Tour Divide dream, were in jeopardy.

Thanks to the nimble hands of Carlos the "Magic Man," a house-calling Thai masseur, I returned to full activity by mid-January. Lamentably, the fear of re-injury overpowered me. Prudence thus dictated switching my bike selection to a rig offering comfort over efficiency and I chose a used Salsa Timberjack 27.5*plus* (27.5" referring to tire diameter/size; *plus* referring to the larger width of the tires). The Timberjack offered front-suspension. The plus-sized tires offered forgiveness in rough terrain. To be safe, I also added additional accessories for enhanced comfort including a Thudbuster suspension seat-post for more cushion, a Brooks B-17 leather saddle for sit-bone comfort, and a Jones H-Bar handlebar for more upright riding posture (as the H-Bar handlebars sweep back at a 45 degree angle toward the rider rather than straight sideways from the stem). Another significant positive with the Timberjack is a large triangle opening in its main frame that is ideal for stowing a large triangular frame bag.

Sorry, the gear info is probably TMI for most readers.

In early March, I ordered a whistle. This was only noteworthy as my final major purchase item for the Tour Divide. Do not laugh. I used that damn whistle at several important moments on the Tour. The same day I ordered the whistle, I also bought a plane ticket to Calgary and booked lodging for the nights preceding the race. Logistically, I was prepared. With three months to go, I just had to ensure that my body and mind would be prepared.

A comprehensive description of Tour Divide training would require several chapters . . . and would send the majority of readers to sleep or to the next book on their reading lists. I will therefore summarize my training in a few paragraphs. I did not follow a formal training plan. I merely mirrored the informal Leadville regimen that I followed each winter.

Once my back healed in late January, I spent eight weeks building endurance with three 90-minute sessions per week riding indoors on a Schwinn spin-bike. The main progression was extending the amount of time I could maintain a "standing-climb" at a moderate heart rate at 65 rpm (revolutions per minute). By late March, I could stand on the pedals for 40 minutes straight.

I devoted one day each week to lifting weights in the gym and one day performing long hill-repeats on my fully loaded bike in the mountains 45 minutes west of Washington D.C.. A hill repeat is as simple as it sounds: climb a hill, preferably one with at least 800 feet of elevation gain, cruise back to the bottom and do it again . . . and again . . . and again.

Some racers swear by long training blocks consisting of riding 60+ miles per day for at least three or four consecutive days. I opted out of training blocks. I was escaping life for four to five weeks for this race. That was enough. My plan was to show up at the starting line in decent shape and simply ride myself into full fitness during the first week of the race. The only real "block" I built was a two-day 160-mile overnight ride in late April, the primary purpose of which was not fitness, but to test my sleep system and to see how I would handle camping alone for the first time in my life. Hell, I had not camped since I was in my early 20s!

Luckily, I had no issues.

I continued my indoor workouts the first two weeks of May and then heeded the advice of many Tour veterans and did not ride at all during the last three weeks before the Tour so that my body was fresh at the start. As the race approached, I had no sense whether my informal training regimen sufficed. Thinking back to all of the mistakes that I made during my maiden Leadville experience in 2007, I was sure that I was sinking knee-deep in a bog of Tour rookie errors. Nevertheless, I figured that the Tour was long enough that I could learn on the fly and overcome those mistakes.

Curiously, I strategically avoided training in inclement weather. Though I was certain to face atrocious weather conditions at various times during the race, I concluded that no toughness gained from suffering miserably during training rides was worth dampening (literally and figuratively) my enthusiasm for the adventure.

By mid-May, I was physically as ready as I could be. My mental readiness turned out to be a whole 'nuther story.

Chapter 5 – "Money, get away, get a good job with good
pay and you're okay;
Money, it's a gas, grab that cash with both
hands and make a stash;
New car, caviar, four star daydream, think
I'll buy me a football team"
— Pink Floyd, *Money*

The smile of good fortune placed me in position to ride the Tour Divide. Most people my age do not have the time or career flexibility to fly (or bike) off the grid for four to six weeks. My kids were old enough that Lisa could ably handle all parenting duties in my absence. On the career front, I am a self-employed business and transactional attorney and have the luxury of managing workflow without the stress of meeting hourly quotas, satisfying bosses and/or partners, or scheduling court appearances. I joke with my litigation colleagues that I barely know the difference between a courthouse and outhouse. There is a difference, right?

The weeks prior to the Tour were spent closing out projects and making my clients aware of my impending hiatus. All were supportive.

The fundraiser for First Descents emerged as the most meaningful financial facet of the Tour Divide. I spent most of April crafting and re-crafting the perfect solicitation email, and worked with the tireless Andrew "Tops" Coulter, Development Coordinator at First Descents, to create an appealing fundraising web page. Six weeks before the Tour, we 'went live' with both the email solicitation and the donation webpage. The initial publicized fundraising goal was an ambitious $150,000. The first paragraph of my donation page read as follows:

> *"Meet First Descents' Board Chairman Brent Goldstein. Brent would like to raise an obscene amount of money for First Descents, a nonprofit that provides life-changing outdoor adventures for young adults impacted by cancer. To do so, Brent is blending a dash of mid-life crisis with a pinch of stupidity and a bucketful of heart into a carb-infused smoothie known as the Tour Divide challenge. The Tour Divide challenge is simple: Race the rooftop of North America by mountain bike; travel self-supported along all 2,731 miles of the off-road Great Divide (i.e., Continental Divide) Mountain Bike Route; keep moving, be moved, battle physical, mental and emotional demons (and wildlife); eat when hungry,*

drink when thirsty, pitch a tent when tired and DO NOT QUIT; finish as fast as possible without help and without cracking. The Tour Divide requires no designated rest periods or set distances a racer must travel daily. The clock runs non-stop starting with a "Grand Depart" from Banff, Alberta at 8am on June 8th and finishing at the US border crossing at Antelope Wells, New Mexico some 3-5 weeks later. Tour Divide is the longest and arguably most challenging mountain bike time trial on the planet. It is a challenge for the ultra-fit and the ultra-insane, but only if ultra-prepared for the myriad contingencies and challenges of long-distance backcountry biking."

The outright outlandishness of this challenge must have resonated as generous donations immediately poured in along with a string of heartfelt and supportive comments from donors. In addition to cash donations, several friends pledged amounts ranging from 10 cents per mile to two dollars per mile with some offering double and triple bonuses if I had the temerity to finish the race. The incredible response from the community buoyed me (and downright frightened me when I considered my exposure to reciprocal donation requests!).

Within two weeks, the fundraiser achieved $60,000. Ten days later, it had jumped to $95,000. By my departure date, the total reached $140,000 in combined cash donations and pledged amounts. Before leaving, I increased the fundraising goal from $150,000 to $200,000. That the decision to attempt an asinine bike race could have such a material impact on people's lives — in this case the lives of young cancer survivors — was astonishing. The overwhelming generosity of my peers filled me with pride and equipped me with ironclad determination.

Chapter 6 – "Cause I'm leavin' on a jet plane, Don't know when I'll be back again"
— John Denver, *Leaving on a Jet Plane*

As departure day approached, I unexpectedly found myself on shaky emotional ground. During the 12 months preceding the Tour Divide, the race was an amorphous concept murkily suspended on the horizon. Although I had purchased all of the gear, worked out all of the travel plans, and completed all of my training, the Tour did not seem real. It was a romantic dream. I was not really going to ride a mountain bike 2700+ miles down the Continental Divide. Seriously, why would anyone do that? It's preposterous.

I do not think reality hit Lisa or my daughters until two weeks prior to takeoff. In a fit of pique, my oldest daughter (23 year-old Daryn) called Lisa from New York asking, "Mom, how in the world could you let Dad do this?!"

Lisa responded, "Where have you been for the last 8 months?"

My middle daughter (19 year-old Arlyn), fresh home from her first year of college, peppered me with an onslaught of questions about bears and mountain-lions and frost-bite and bike crashes and broken bones and how I could possibly come out of this alive. Great pep talk Arlyn!

My youngest daughter's (16 year-old Bailey) piercing blue eyes filled with fear and disbelief whenever we discussed the race.

During all of my planning, researching and excitement, I failed to fully realize how my decision to race the Tour Divide affected my loved ones. A tsunami of guilt induced by these 11th-hour conversations washed over me. Worse, the selfishness of the endeavor was painfully crystallized. What if I suffered some life-altering or life-ending mishap in the wilderness? Why should my wife and daughters suffer for my foolishness?

Exacerbating my emotional turmoil was the fact that the Washington Capitals were in the Stanley Cup Finals. How is this relevant? Well your honor, indulge me to lay some evidentiary foundation. My Dad took me to my first Capitals' game in 1974 when they were an expansion team. One game hooked me for life. My Dad purchased season tickets and I started playing hockey. I still play two nights a week and we are in our 45th year of season-ticket die-hard fandom. I do not say that proudly. I often wished I could walk away.

Washington Caps' fans are an abused collective of Wile E. Coyotes with lives annually tormented by playoff heartache, disappointment and zero Stanley Cup championships. No other team snatched defeat from the jaws of victory as adeptly as our Washington Capitals. But this year was different. The Caps overcame adversity, won three playoff series and were suddenly four games away from winning the most hallowed trophy in sports for the first time in their history.

For those who scoff at team sports and at the fans who devote such passion and loyalty to their chosen teams, you simply do not get it. Attempting to explain it is also pointless, as you still will not get it. Fandom is irrational and silly, but when playoff time comes (or tournament time in college) the emotion is real, the excitement and stress are palpable, nerves fray, and blood pressure spikes. Sports often unite families and communities more fervently than politics, religion and/or culture.

Over the course of my life, hockey games and football games provided some of the strongest and most memorable bonding experiences with my dad and my daughters. I live in a city (Washington D.C.) where everyone disagrees about everything and where political, ethnic and economic lines are clearly drawn. In late spring of 2018, a professional hockey team united my city and I was likely to be literally lost in the wilderness when the magical moment of victory arrived.

I suffered from a severe case of cognitive dissonance. Though flushed with excitement for the start of the Tour Divide and a possible Stanley Cup victory, I felt glum that I would not be around to share such a "life-moment" victory with my wife, dad and daughters. The rational side of my brain told me to "get the hell over it." However, the rational side of my brain also looked the other way when I decided to race the Tour Divide. The rational side of my brain had thus lost all credibility and influence long ago!

I battled with these conflicting emotions every minute of every day in the week before departure and was a tearful wreck by the time Lisa dropped me off at BWI Airport on Wednesday morning, June 6. WTF? I have an even-keeled persona and usually have no trouble corralling my emotions. Untethered emotion was uncharted territory for me, and quite unsettling. Maybe I should have gotten Valium along with my prescription for steroidal butt cream! By the way, that was not a joke. Steroidal butt cream saved my ass on the Tour.

Forlornly standing at the curb as Lisa drove away, I questioned my fundamental race-philosophy. I purposefully chose to undertake the Tour as a solo adventure. I asked no friends to join me. I had no desire to depend on anyone and less desire to have anyone depend on me. Hitting me like a proverbial bag of frozen steaks at that moment was how completely and uncomfortably alone I felt. Ironically, the one person who would have been the perfect partner on this journey was Al.

During all of the months of preparations and mental machinations, I never envisioned such a depressing departure for the adventure of a lifetime. I shook my fist at the sky and muttered, "Screw you, Al!" and walked into the airport. Al and his stupid phone call and his stupid cancer and his stupid death were clearly the blame for all of this.

I could not get a direct flight from Washington to Calgary. Ironically, I routed through Denver (ironic because First Descents' headquarters is located in Denver). While retrieving my luggage at the Denver baggage claim during my layover, Ray Shedd, First Descents' Director of Development, and Andrew Coulter, First Descents' Development Coordinator, accosted me boisterously.

"Heeeeey Brent!" bellowed Ray from 100 feet away.

"Ray and Andrew, what the hell are you guys doing here?" I asked with a huge grin as they approached.

Both gave me robust man-hugs before Ray responded, "Brent, a little birdie told us of your layover in Denver. The least we could do was drive out here to give you big 'ole bear-hugs and a proper send-off."

Ray then reached into a bag and pulled out a string of multi-colored Tibetan prayer flags with messages of love and encouragement from all of the First Descents' staff. Just when I thought that I had finally flat-lined my emotions, tears flowed in the baggage claim area. Jeez, I needed to start riding my damn bike already! This emotional crap was KILLING me.

I arrived in Calgary later that afternoon. Gratefully, the box containing my bike also arrived with me . . . and without any holes or dents! I met several other Tour Divide racers in the Calgary customs line and all had the same looks of anxiety that I felt. One guy from Colorado returned for his third try at the race after failing to finish the prior two times (he failed again). Another Coloradan was back for his fourth stab after three unsuccessful attempts (he finished). A guy from Ohio admitted that he was so petrified that he nearly cancelled the trip the night before his flight (he failed to finish). A guy from Georgia said he was only doing the race to lose 30 pounds and suspected that he would have been better off simply dieting (I think he failed at both finishing AND losing the weight). A guy from Australia said, "G'day mate" and shuffled off.

From Calgary, I took a shuttle to Canmore, Alberta. Although the race started from Banff in two days, when I tried back in March to book two nights in Banff, there were no hotels available the first night. No big deal. Canmore was only a 20-mile bike ride from Banff. Staying in Canmore the first night and riding to Banff the following day allowed me to simulate the three major components of a Tour Divide day: departure, ride, and arrival. The ride to Banff also provided me with the opportunity to ensure that everything on the bike was working okay after spending the last two days in a cardboard box getting jostled by airport baggage handlers. Most importantly, the ride from Canmore to Banff introduced me to the incredible grandeur of the Canadian Rockies. The beautiful ride and the breathtaking views helped clear the voluminous emotional detritus that had accumulated in my brain over the prior few weeks. With each mile, my focus shifted closer to tomorrow and farther from yesterday.

    I arrived in Banff at noon and my hotel was not ready until 3PM. I rode south to inspect the first five miles of the Tour route and then returned to a coffee shop in town to meet my friend Grace Ragland. I met Grace several years ago in Leadville and we distantly followed each other's lives on Facebook, with both learning sometime in the fall of 2017 that we were each racing the Tour Divide. Grace's story is amazing. She is 56 years old, and has battled and overcome multiple sclerosis since she was a teenager. She is an accomplished mountain bike racer and, like me, yearned to engage in the ultimate test and adventure. As two Tour Divide rookies, we stayed in constant contact through the winter, comparing notes and ideas as well as fears and concerns. Though I was racing solo, it was beneficial to communicate with someone else going through the same experience. Grace and I hung out for 45 minutes and compared final notes. I then took off to do some shopping as I still needed bear spray, sunblock, a pair of wool socks, and food and water for Day 1 of the race.

    After shopping, I checked into the Bow View Lodge and then walked over to Banff's main street needing to accomplish one last huge task. That evening was Game 5 of the Stanley Cup. The Caps had a three-to-one series lead and I fervently hoped that Game 5 would be the clincher. My task was to find a bar that would not only show the game on a big-screen HDTV, but would broadcast the game audio. Just about every bar fit that bill. This was Canada, for Pete's sake!

    At 5PM, I attended an unofficial racer meeting at a pizza joint downtown. I stayed an hour and listened to race advice from an entertaining and wildly energetic Banff relic named "Crazy Larry." Crazy Larry held no official role or title, but his love for the Tour Divide over the years made him the unofficial send-off spokesperson/storyteller/greeter/pep-talker/advice-dispenser for the race. I tried to give my full attention to Crazy Larry, but my focus was squarely on the hockey game (and on my watch as I counted down the minutes until puck-drop).

    I left the pizza place at 6PM and made my way to a bar aptly named the

"Brew Pub."

A few days before I left for Canada, I scrolled through the racer entries and discovered that two other Washington D.C. guys were signed up for the race. I emailed them and asked if they wanted to meet me to watch Game 5. Both responded yes and showed up at the Brew Pub a few minutes before the game started. One was a 64-year old ex-military machine named Mitch and the other was a young guy (late 20s) named Ben. Through brief introductions and small talk, I learned that Mitch was a Tour Divide veteran. In retrospect, Mitch would have been an amazing Tour Divide resource for me. Unfortunately, Mitch had never before watched a hockey game. As such, except for pleasantries exchanged during commercials, I was piss-poor company for Mitch due to my fierce fixation on the game. Mitch would go on to crush the Tour Divide, finishing in 22 days.

Ben was a fellow first-time racer with many self-doubts, but he was a Caps fan, so we at least shared in the excitement of the moment. In hindsight, maybe Ben should have spent less time watching hockey and more time talking race strategy with Mitch. Ben scratched from the race on Day 3.

The hockey game was edge-of-seat intense from the opening face-off. The Caps trailed 3-2 at the second intermission when Mitch took his leave from the bar. His departure was relieving as his presence as a non-hockey fan fell somewhere between distracting and irritating (through no fault of his own). I was so nervous during the third period that I could barely speak. The Caps tied the game with ten minutes left in the third and then took the lead two minutes later as I self-ejected from the barstool, practically knocking over a table. The tourists in the bar looked at me in amusement. Most people were barely paying attention to the game. It was bizarre (and a buzz-kill) to watch the most momentous game of my life in an atmosphere permeated by indifference.

When the final buzzer sounded and the Washington Capitals were the Stanley Cup champions, I cried for about the tenth time that week. Reflecting my conflicting emotions, these were tears of boundless joy mixed with tears of melancholy. I was on Cloud 10 for winning the Cup, but wistful about not sharing this incredible life-moment with those most important to me. It was nice to give Ben a hug and a high-five, but our history together was all of three hours and I would never see him again.

I remained in my seat to watch the post-game interviews and presentation of the Stanley Cup and nearly lost my mind when the bar, within seconds of the game ending, switched the audio to live Madonna karaoke. Seriously? In Canada? And Madonna? Fortunately, I did not need sound to read the lips of Caps' captain Alex Ovechkin when NHL commissioner Gary Bettman handed him the Stanley Cup. Of course, tears streamed from my eyes once again. Now I was fully convinced that Lisa secretly injected me with estrogen three weeks before I left! Pathetic.

   I settled the tab, called Lisa as I left the bar, and excitedly conversed with her for my 15-minute walk back to the hotel. We discussed the game for a few minutes and then shifted gears to the little bike race that I would be starting at 8AM the next morning. Holy shit! I would be racing the Tour Divide when I awoke! For three hours that evening, I barely thought about the race beyond those few fleeting moments when Mitch successfully engaged me.

   Just before going to sleep, I completed the remaining tasks on my to-do list by changing my voicemail greeting and the auto-response on my email. Both messages essentially said to leave me alone for the next month. The time had arrived to leave the world behind and just go ride my bike!

Chapter 7 – "I want to ride my bicycle,
I want to ride my bike
I want to ride my bicycle,
I want to ride it where I like"
— Queen, *Bicycle Race*

June 8, 2018 - Tour Divide Day 1 - 100 Miles from Banff, Alberta to Elkford, British Columbia. I awoke at 6:30AM after a restless night of sleep littered with outrageous dreams. In one dream, the Washington Capitals were the Stanley Cup champions. In another, I was at the start line of a mountain bike race that spanned over 2700 miles. Like I said, outrageous dreams. Oh wait!

After coming to grips with my twin realities, I loaded my bike, checked out of the hotel, rode to a nearby deli for a breakfast sandwich, and then coasted to the Banff YWCA for the 8AM Grand Depart. I dearly hoped that the emotional roller coaster that I had ridden for the past few weeks would end the second I started pedaling south from the Y.

I leaned my bike against a fence fronting the Y and scanned the gathering crowd for a familiar face. Not recognizing anyone, I crossed the street and sat on a grassy embankment to gather my final thoughts. I was excited, anxious and petrified. The excited side of me just wanted to GO GO GO. The anxious, petrified side of me repeatedly asked what the hell I had gotten myself into.

At 7:45AM, all of the riders posed for a picture while listening to an intro speech by "Crazy Larry." His wisest advice was, "If you see a bear . . . take a picture!"

Brilliant!

In addition to Crazy Larry, quite a cast of characters surrounded me. One guy wore a tutu. One guy mounted two guitars on the back of his bike and planned to play concerts along the route. One woman dressed as a princess, and one guy strapped a large take-out pizza box to his back (presumably filled with a full pizza).

The race officially began at 8AM with a rather anticlimactic start. I expected a gun, siren, or at least a collective primal group scream. Instead, we matter-of-factly mounted our bikes and slowly rolled south on the paved road. When we reached the trailhead a few minutes later, I pushed the "start" button on my bike computer and marveled that I would not press "stop" until I either quit the race or arrived at the Mexico border in Antelope Wells, New Mexico some 2,731 miles later.

Day 1 rewarded us with picture-perfect weather — partly sunny, high temperatures in the 70s and a light breeze. Unfortunately, drastic changes were in store as the weatherman predicted cold, rainy, and possibly even snowy conditions for the coming days. Relying on the poor futurecast, I made my first rookie mistake. My original strategy, forged over the previous four months, was to start the race slowly with 75 to 80 miles on Day 1 and another 75 to 80 miles on Day 2. Thinking that I should take advantage of the good weather, I cavalierly made an 11th-hour change to my carefully formulated plan and, before leaving Banff, booked a hotel room in Elkford 100 miles from the start. This was a dumb decision for reasons that will later become evident.

The first 30 to 35 miles were on a beautiful undulating wooded trail that meandered and rolled south from Banff. After months of planning and overthinking and worrying, I was finally "free to be" and commencing a process of nearly unmitigated disconnection. I had no idea how often I would have mobile service over the next month and I did not care. I would not follow the news, I would disengage from political drama, and I would barely think of work or house problems or television or the economy or bills or any of the other typical stresses or concerns that fill the average person's cranium on a daily basis.

At the 20-mile mark, I spied a female racer ahead with a braided blond ponytail cascading below her helmet. As the distance narrowed between us, I realized that it was Grace. She was feeling ill when we met in Banff the day before and I hoped that riding was her antidote.

Pulling up alongside her, I asked, "Hey Grace, how ya doing so far?"

Grace responded in surprise, "Brent! I was wondering where you were. I thought you would be way out in front of me. I'm still feeling a bit crappy but am so happy to be out here. Isn't this amazing?"

"It is crazy beautiful out here," I answered. "I got a bit waylaid at the start as I couldn't get my bike computer to work and am still having some issues. For now, I'm just following the crowd."

We rode together and chitchatted for about ten miles until the wooded trail spit us out on a gravel road. Grace took a quick break at the turn-off and I continued.

A few miles later, a guy slowly passed me who looked faintly familiar. I rode up next to him and exclaimed, "Hey, I voted for you for President the last two elections!"

He laughed aloud and said, "Thanks!"

It was none other than former New Mexico Governor and twice Independent Presidential Candidate, Gary Johnson. I rode with Gary for an hour talking a little bit about politics and a lot about the race. He also tried to help me figure out the navigation function on my bike computer. I could see the red line on the screen that denoted the race-route, but the little triangle that is supposed to represent my position kept scrolling down off the screen. Seriously, what kind of moron shows up at the start of an adventure like this and does not know how to use his bike computer? At least Gary was getting a glimpse into the brain capacity of one of his typical voters. Maybe that is why he could not win! Well, that and Aleppo.

At about mile 45, we turned off the gravel road onto an exhilarating single-track trail that swooped up and down and in and out of a thick forest for ten miles and included a dramatic ravine crossing over a narrow suspension bridge. During that stretch, I lost Gary (never to be seen by me again), but had a blast. Unfortunately, that stretch of single-track contained a series of short steep rises and descents that triggered mild leg cramps. Really? I have had a checkered history with cramping on long rides, particularly on hot days, but I had not cramped once all spring. Luckily, I was a seasoned expert at managing cramps and was able to continue pedaling by shifting to my least resistant gears.

At mile 60 I arrived at the first resupply point of the Tour Divide, a campground grocery store called Boulton Creek. My legs were feeling achy by then and it occurred to me that I had taken Day 1 for granted. For one, I did not account for altitude. I was riding terrain that was a mile above sea level and was not acclimated. Moreover, I did not factor the cumulative elevation gain for Day 1. Although there were no single monster climbs, I had still aggregated nearly 5,000 feet of elevation gain by the time I reached Boulton Creek. Finally, I woefully planned my nutrition and hydration for Day 1. In short, I did not eat enough food (particularly food with sodium) or drink nearly enough fluids. Even dumber, I did not supplement my water with any electrolytes. Rookie, rookie, rookie!

In all of my one-day races and lengthy rides, I consumed all of my calories, nutrition, hydration and electrolytes from powdered formulas mixed with water. Carrying large quantities of powders is impossible on the Tour Divide. I mistakenly assumed that since I would rarely be pedaling at a hard "race-pace," my body would quickly get used to a mixture of water and off-the-convenience-store-shelf calories. I also mistakenly figured that I could survive by drinking less than the 24-30 ounces per hour of fluids that I typically consumed in a race. I took nearly seven hours to get to Boulton Creek. My total fluid intake at that point consisted of a measly 72 ounces. That is barely ten ounces per hour. It is no wonder that the rookie was cramping and tired.

From Boulton Creek, the route took a turn upward onto our first sustained climb of the Tour and our first crossing of the Continental Divide at Elk Pass. After cresting the pass, the route continued for 30 miles on Elk River Road, a swooping dirt road with dramatic craggy snow-capped peaks towering above to the right and left.

Late in the afternoon, I caught up to a woman on Elk River Road who shared that she was racing the Tour Divide for the second consecutive year after being forced to quit the prior year in Pie Town, New Mexico, just 375 miles from the finish. Her name was Jacki, she was roughly my age, and she hailed from somewhere in Wyoming.

"Wow," I commented. "That must have sucked having to quit so close to the finish."

"Brent, you have no idea," Jacki answered. "I had been sucking down Advils like candy for days on end to combat muscle soreness and finally my stomach just gave out. It would have been too dangerous to continue and I made the smart decision."

"Jacki, sorry to hear that, but it is pretty cool that you are able to come back and try again. I hope you make it to the end this time."

"Yeah, me too," responded Jacki with optimism. "Every year, there are dozens of racers who can't live with their prior failure on the Tour and spend the next year, sometimes years, thinking of nothing but returning to 'get the monkey off the back.' I am one of those poor saps. And if I fail again, I'll be back next year."

While the two of us were chatting, we missed a turn and I had my first of many experiences with the dreaded blue line on my Garmin computer. When correctly following the route, the colored triangle that represents me should always sit atop a graphic red line that constitutes the race route. A deviation from the prescribed route triggers a blue line that illustrates the path between the situs of the missed turn and the current location of the triangle. With luck, one discovers their mistake quickly and painlessly retraces the path. We noticed our mistake within a half-mile, turned around and found the turn we missed.

I rode with Jacki for another half-hour, but her plan was to stop and camp near mile 85. As afternoon was turning to evening, I said goodbye and took off for Elkford as I hoped to arrive there before 9PM.

I should have stayed with Jacki.

The town of Elkford is located three miles beyond the route turn-off toward a five-mile climb called "Koko Claims." When I shot past the Koko Claims turn-off, the blue line on my Garmin appeared for the second time that day. At least this time was by design. I arrived in Elkford at 9PM feeling sore and spent. I quietly asked myself whether I could really do this every day for the next 27 to 30 days. I also admonished myself for taking so lightly a 100-mile ride on the first day.

While checking in to the somewhat seedy Elkford Motor Inn, there was another rider at the counter who arrived a few minutes ahead of me. The hotel desk clerk just informed him that there was no vacancy. Overhearing the conversation, I asked the clerk whether my room contained two beds. When he responded yes, I looked at the rider and said, "Hey man, I'd be happy to split my room with you. I'm Brent."

He looked at me with a tired grin and responded, "Brent, you are a lifesaver. Thanks so much! I'm Mike."

I figured my invitation was a good opportunity to start the race on the positive side of the karma ledger!

I threw my stuff in the room, took a quick shower, and went down to the restaurant/bar. I then ate a barely edible pizza and chicken tenders for dinner, sent Lisa a quick text letting her know that I was alive and in one piece, headed back to the room, bid goodnight to Mike and blissfully fell asleep.

Crazy Larry – Tour orator

Group photo - That's me top right

As clean as I'll be for the next month

Suspension bridge

Beauty

Wild horses

Chapter 8 – "I'm on the highway to hell, on the highway to hell."
— **AC/DC,** *Highway to Hell*

Tour Divide Day 2 - 73 Miles - Elkford, British Columbia to Fernie, British Columbia. I awoke at 6:30AM feeling disoriented and lightheaded. I was sore, tired and dehydrated from the previous day, but desired an early start to tackle the Koko Claims monster. Tour veterans universally proclaim Koko Claims to be the Tour Divide's meanest, toughest, most soul-crushing section. Before leaving the motel, I filled two 24-ounce bottles and a two-liter plastic bottle with water. Although there were streams along the climb where I could refill the bottles, I wanted to be doubly sure that I carried enough water after my failure to hydrate properly the day before.

After checking out and saying farewell to Mike, I left the motel, backtracked the three miles from Elkford to the Koko Claims turnoff, and rejoined the red line. I started the climb by pedaling in my easiest gear to warm up and shake the cobwebs out of my legs (and the clichés out of my brain). Dense cloud-cover enveloped the trail and chilly 40-degree temperatures penetrated my outer clothing layers. Cold rain was imminent.

The first two miles after the turn-off were mostly rideable. Maybe the prolific horror stories describing this climb were exaggerations. Maybe the climb consisted of a series of intermittent hikes interspersed with rideable sections. I could handle that. Maybe the whole Tour Divide was really just a two-wheeled spin through daisy fields and chocolate trees! As I continued to pedal, a feeling of false confidence — even false bravado — overtook me. I was about to learn that on the Tour Divide, false confidence is both a kicker of asses and a squasher of psyches.

The outskirts of Delusionville ended abruptly when I rounded a bend in the trail and met face-to-face with a steep menacing wall of rocks. Forward momentum carried me a few feet up the rocky incline before having to dismount and push upward on foot. The ascent continued for a quarter mile before slightly leveling, only to quickly and sharply rise again . . . and again . . . and again. After 45 minutes and thinking it could not get worse, it got worse, a lot worse.

Heavy winter snows spawned multiple avalanches that covered the trail with rocks, snow and fallen trees. The first avalanche zone extended the length of a football field and required both dexterity and strength to push and lift a fully loaded beast of a bike up, over, through and around the debris. Once through the debris pile, Mother Nature laughed and gave a quick clockwise turn to the cold knob on the rain faucet. Minutes later, the rain turned to hail. Growling profanity, I labored over several more steep rises of rocky trail and two additional hulking dumps of avalanche debris. It was horrendous beyond anything imaginable.

Hike-a-bike does not intimidate me. I have toiled through plenty of hike-a-bike in my mountain biking life. However, Koko Claims won the malevolence grand prize. The best way to describe the Koko Claims experience is as follows: imagine sitting on an upright bench-press, setting the weight at 58 pounds, and then pressing 2,000 times. Do this in a refrigerator . . . one that spits out hail and mist and rain. And make sure you exercised for 13 hours the day before. And make sure you are dehydrated because you royally messed up your prior day's fluid intake. And finally, make sure you coat the floor with a foot of toothpaste to mimic the feeling of sinking in soft snow. Oh wait, one last thing. Breathe exclusively through a straw to simulate the reduced oxygen found 7,000 feet above sea level. Having fun yet?

One mile from the summit and almost two hours into this nonsense, I finished the second of my two 24-ounce bottles. Reaching down to grab the two-liter bottle attached to a cage on the bike's front fork, I horrifically discovered an empty bottle thanks to a crack in the plastic. Adding insult to injury, due to the consistently precipitous slope, there were no further creek crossings and thus no ability to filter water. At this point, I was compounding the dehydration from the day before with a new shortage of fluids, all while burning calories at a dizzying rate.

Fuuuuuck!

I had no great options. Sitting down and resting risked hypothermia. Turning around and descending this abomination of a trail risked a horrific crash. Push, brake, step. Push, brake, step. Push, brake, step. Eyes down. Do not slip. Concentrate. Mutter incoherently. Push, brake, step. Push, brake, step. Push, brake, step.

I finally reached the summit after three hours of torturous climbing and profuse cursing. Like an oasis in a desert, a cabin was nestled among the pines at the top. The grass surrounding the cabin was home to a haphazard array of abandoned bikes. I carelessly let my bike fall into the grass, climbed a set of stairs, and burst through the front door of the cabin. Inside the cabin were seven equally miserable bikers, each of whom possessed equally miserable sunken eyes and equally far off gazes. I was soaking wet, dizzy, frazzled and my fingers and toes were numb. I plopped myself down onto a bench and exhaled heavily. Desperately needing water, a long stay was imprudent. I just needed to gather my wits. I considered asking another racer for a swig of water. However, the rules of the race prohibit taking supplies from fellow riders. It was only Day 2 and I was not about to break the rules . . . yet. That would come soon enough. Thankfully, one of the other cabin denizens assured me that multiple creeks crossed the trail within a few minutes of descending from the cabin.

I left the cabin after an all-too-short rest and began my descent. There was a stream crossing a quarter mile down. Hallellujah! This was my first time using my special filtration solution. A person of average intelligence would have familiarized himself with the instructions on the two solution bottles labeled A and B before the race. Not this jackass. To borrow a catchphrase from my childhood idol Maxwell Smart, "That's what they would be expecting me to do!" Who is "they?" KAOS? Does not matter. Damn, I was both babbling and dating/aging myself. Sorry about that, Chief.

Digression over, I quickly skimmed the instructions. First, fill the water bottle with stream water. Second, pour eight drops from solution bottle A into the water bottle. Third, pour eight drops from solution bottle B into the water bottle. Fourth, shake everything up and wait 30 minutes for the purifying agents to take effect. Wait, what? 30 minutes?!?! I could not wait another 30 seconds, much less 30 minutes.

I submerged my bottle in the stream, chugged 24 ounces of icy water, submerged the bottle again, and chugged another 24 ounces. Then I submerged the bottle one last time and applied the solution as instructed. Life is all about educated risks or, in this case, uneducated risks. I hoped that an iron coating lined my stomach.

The first part of the descent contained several gnarly steep rocky sections and multiple stream crossings. I was able to ride most of these sections and was successful keeping my feet dry at the first creek crossing. Unfortunately, the next several streams were either too wide, too deep, or contained water flowing too furiously to ride through. Crankily, I gritted my teeth and waded through the icy water with fully submerged feet. After a few miles of white-knuckled descending, the trail leveled out and continued through a lush forest before widening into an old logging road that would gradually descend another 50 miles towards the ski resort town of Fernie, British Columbia (with one big climb and one subsequent big descent into town).

The logging road was damp and soggy from the early morning rains and the surface worsened as I descended. At mile 30, the road turned to quagmire and I spent a good 30 minutes literally stuck in the mud. A peanut-buttery mud caked my tires, my drive train, my pedals and my chain, restraining all forward movement. After clearing the mud from the frame and tires with my numb fingers for the fifth time, I slammed the bike into the weeds on the side of the road in disgust and exasperation.

Laugh, cry or pass out. Those were my options. I was miserable. I was despondent. I was scared. I was numb. I was borderline delirious. I questioned why the hell I had chosen to do this stupid race in the first place. Most of all, my mental weakness pissed me off. Why was I unable to do what I taught my kids to do since birth in tough situations and SUCK IT UP? Where was the flip to switch? I knew the Tour Divide would be hard and uncomfortable, but I did not bargain for abject misery. For the tenth time that day, I bellowed, "FUUUUUUCK!!!"

After wallowing on the side of the road for ten or fifteen minutes with my head buried in my hands, I heard the sounds of an approaching bike. I slowly raised my gaze and recognized the rider as Jacki from the day before. What a vision. She might as well have had a halo over her helmet and wings for arms.

Jacki stopped next to me and asked, "Brent, are you okay?"

I shook my head slowly from side to side and emitted a feeble, "Hey Jacki. No, I'm not good."

Jacki dismounted from her bike and said, "You look really pale. What have you been eating and drinking over the last 24 hours?"

I slowly told my somber tale about the cracked bottle, the general lack of water, and the failure to use electrolytes the first day. Jacki unhesitatingly reached into her backpack, grabbed a handful of electrolyte tablets and salt pills, and literally force-fed me. Officially, this was Tour Divide rule violation number 1. Screw the rules.

Jacki handed me two electrolyte tablets to insert in a bottle of water. While waiting for the tablets to dissolve, Jacki inserted another two tabs directly into my mouth with an order to chew and swallow them. A minute later, I chugged the contents of the water bottle. Finally, she asked if I had any protein bars. Nodding affirmatively, Jacki instructed me to "quickly eat two of them now." I quickly ate two of them then.

I did not suddenly spring to life like Marty McFly at the Enchantment Under the Sea Dance in the movie *Back to the Future*. However, I quickly felt better under Jacki's patient and generous care (thank you Jacki wherever you are!) and mustered the strength to fight through the rest of the muddy section. Jacki stayed with me for another two hours to confirm that I was okay, and then I pedaled the remaining miles alone to the town of Fernie where I made a beeline for the first hotel on the left (Best Western of Fernie).

Walking into the Best Western, I felt lower than low. Still a bit nauseous and light-headed, I reflected on the danger of being alone and unable to get help, and I again questioned my sanity and my ability to make rational decisions . . . such as deciding beforehand that the Tour Divide was a colossally dumbshit idea! To make matters worse, the two-day forecast for southern British Columbia consisted of cold rain, mixed precipitation and higher-elevation snow.

After checking in at the front desk, I heaved my bike into a hotel storage closet, ambled dejectedly to my room, tossed all of my disgusting clothes into the bathtub, called Lisa, and begged her to find me the next shuttle to the nearest airport. Two days in and I was DONE. The hardest bike race in the world claimed an early victim.

I love my wife. She sacrificed significantly for me to partake in this adventure and she was not about to let me make a rash decision in a pique of emotion. With a tone of admonishment, Lisa said, "Who is this? It certainly is not my husband! Stop babbling for a minute and listen to me. I want you to take a hot shower, get some food, have a beer or two, and call me back."

While in the shower, she summoned the cavalry in the form of my buddies Kevin Kane and Jeff Hoffman and urged them reach out to give me pep-texts about why I was doing this race (i.e., my charity fundraiser) and why quitting was not an option. Once clean, I donned dry clothes and went downstairs to eat dinner at the hotel restaurant. I ordered a heaping plate of lasagna and a pint of beer and read a spate of texts from Lisa, Kevin and Jeff containing words of encouragement and support. With a full stomach and marginally better attitude, I sent them all messages assuring them that I had 'come in off the ledge' and was going to sleep mildly confident that tomorrow would be a better day. Kevin's final text was spot-on:

> *"You had poor weather, a huge hike-bike section, ran out of water, etc. It was a shitty day. PERIOD. There is nothing normal about this race. It is a distinct departure from your routine, your comfort level and experience. It will take some adjustment. It is unrealistic to think you would have fun right away. You will have fun. It will come. Tomorrow it gets better. Small bites. Remember tomorrow."*

He is a good man that Kevin Kane. I was sound asleep before 9PM.

Koko Claims hike

Koko Claims avalanche debris

Looking back at avalanche crossing

Feeling a little better

Funny sign approaching Fernie

Chapter 9 – "I hope the day will be a lighter highway,
For friends are found on every road
Can you ever think of any better way
For the lost and weary travelers to go?"
— Elton John, *Friends*

Tour Divide Day 3 - 47 Miles from Fernie, B.C. to Butts Cabin, Flathead Valley, B.C. I woke up on Day 3 at 6:30AM after sleeping for over nine and a half straight hours. For context, I usually sleep six to seven hours a night and never more than eight hours. Evidently, the first two days took a bite out of me. Despite an abundance of sleep, I still felt queasy and weak. Additionally, I felt very alone, very nervous about proceeding, and very doubtful about my ability or desire to complete the race. Completing this disgraceful circle of self-pity, I was woefully unmotivated to set out by myself into the cold rain and snow and, even worse, camp out by myself in the cold rain and snow . . . in grizzly-bear country no less.

One hundred seven miles separated Fernie from the United States border, followed by another nine miles to Eureka, Montana, the next town with full services and indoor accommodations. In between was nothing but muddy roads, thousands of feet of arduous climbing, large wild animals that wanted to eat me, and a miserable weather forecast. Covering that distance in one day would have required a 4AM departure, but that ship sailed . . . at 4AM. Duh.

Before pulling back the bed covers, I reviewed the Tour maps and discovered a shorter option for the day that would entail 47 miles of riding and ending at a rustic public cabin called Butts Cabin. Maybe that should be my plan. I called Lisa and she encouraged me to get my ass moving. She feared that the longer I sat in the hotel room, the more likely I might spend the day bellied up to the hotel bar. I threw on shorts and a t-shirt and took the elevator down for breakfast.

While eating, I sat next to a French-Canadian father and son who were poring over the race maps. They seemed equally unmotivated to leave the hotel. Idle small talk divulged that they likewise endured misery battling Koko Claims and did not arrive in Fernie until nearly 10PM the night before. They continued their discussion in French, and I returned to my room to evaluate and strategize.

Put-up or shut-up time had arrived. My prior evening's angst had largely dissipated, and the excessive sleep combined with a hot breakfast improved my state of mind. A return to "mission mindset" was my top priority. I did not race the Tour Divide merely to challenge the crap out of myself. I had a much deeper purpose. I was racing to financially support and represent a group of young cancer survivors, most of whom would kill for an opportunity (and the health) to attempt an endeavor like the Tour. The ghost of Al was also astride my shoulder and hollering, "Dude, are you hurt? No? Did you lose a limb? No? Did you have to undergo a fucking chemotherapy treatment? NO??? Then quit acting like such a pussy and get back out there!"

I hate spirits. Especially when they are right.

Back in December, I beseeched several First Descents' alumni to share their cancer and First Descents stories with me in written narratives so that I could read them during the Tour for inspiration. I received a couple submissions before throwing out my back, and then cut off the solicitations as I was unsure whether I would even heal enough to start the race. Sitting on the bed that morning in my Fernie hotel room seemed an appropriate time to read one of the stories. Here it is:

> *Dear Sunday[1],*
>
> *At the age of 19, you think you're invincible. Death only happens to other people, mostly old people. When I was 19, I was diagnosed with nasopharyngeal cancer. What if I died before I got to start my life? I met people during treatment who were talking about retirement and I had not even held my first real job yet.*
>
> *They told me I had to have radiation and chemo. I did not know then what radiation was or that it would be so incredibly devastating to my body. I lost some hair, some hearing, most of my taste, my saliva, my ability to eat, and with that, my energy. Some days it would take me 3 hours to eat a meal. There were days that summer when all I did all day was try to get some food in my body while my mouth was covered with mouth sores. I could not even taste good things like ice cream.*
>
> *Although the treatment was hell, it did the job and killed my cancer. I am pretty healthy now and have minimal problems with the lingering side effects.*
>
> *I signed up for a First Descents program five years after I had finished treatment - I thought it would be a nice way to celebrate that anniversary. At first, I was nervous and anxious about meeting all these strangers and going to a "cancer camp."*

---

1   *All First Descents participants, staff and volunteers are bestowed nicknames at the beginning of a program. The purpose behind the nickname concept is to allow participants to leave their cancer identities at home. My nickname is "Sunday." The genesis of that name is a long story for another time.*

> *I am an introvert and was somewhat scared of hanging out with these strangers for a whole week.*
>
> *There is something about getting on the river in your kayak though, which makes you live in the present and let go of your worries. I learned how to paddle through rapids, how to read the river, how to navigate the eddies . . . and I just fell in love with kayaking. As the week went on, I got more and more comfortable in the river, and met each rapid with a smile on my face. Additionally, each day I got more comfortable with my fellow participants and the staff. Through kayaking, we made many unforgettable memories together. It was a relief to meet other people who understood what having cancer meant, who did not judge you, and accepted and supported you. I actually got incredibly sick because of the high altitude and was vomiting for a couple of days during the trip, but it was still one of the best weeks of my life.*
>
> *We made so many amazing memories in just one week of camp that I never want to forget. At one of the campfires, one of our lead-staff members mentioned that at FD we have these amazing communities full of unconditional love handed to us. And it is so true. It was so touching to see the camp staff take care of one of our campers through a series of seizures and make it possible for her to go down the river with us and enjoy the full experience. There were so many precious moments that we shared and that I want to keep in my heart forever.*
>
> *Despite it being a kayaking camp, First Descents was a head fake. We learned how to be confident, how to take challenges head on, how to try new things. We enjoyed the incredibly supportive community and learned to open up, and let our true/best selves shine. We cheered each other on, laughed with each other, and learned how to have fun again. We learned what we are capable of, individually, and together. We became family. I will always look back at FD with awe and wonder how it is able to be so magical every time.*
>
> *Squirt*

I needed to continue for Squirt and countless other Squirts. Unquestionably, there were more bad days and low moments ahead, not to mention melodrama and unprepossessing whining. However, as my friend Kevin pointed out the night before, I survived the worst day possible and things could only improve. I would persevere and drive forward no matter the obstacle.

I called Lisa one more time to tell her that I was leaving. Then I got dressed, tossed my room card on the bed and left the room for good. As an aside, if this adventure is ever adapted to film, the room card floating through the air toward the bed should be captured in slow motion to triumphant musical accompaniment!

While retrieving my bike from the storage room downstairs, I bumped into another racer who was likewise grabbing his bike. Without introduction, he looked across the room at me and remarked, "Tough day out there yesterday, right?"

I nodded in agreement and said, "Yep, worst ever. Koko Claims should be torched, bulldozed and closed to human passage forever!"

He laughed and introduced himself as Wayne from Pittsburgh. Having some fun with him, I shook his hand and said, "Hey Wayne, good to meet you. I'm Brent, I'm from the D.C. area, and I'm lifelong Washington Capitals fan and season-ticket holder." Before he could interject, I added, "One of the great nights of my life was the Caps' knocking your Pittsburgh Penguins out of the playoffs last month!"

Wayne snickered and said, "Congrats Brent! That was a great win. I am a Penguins season-ticket holder and we still have four Stanley Cups to your one!"

Touché Wayne.

Wayne was an overtly friendly and jovial guy and I took an instant liking to him. Although our teams were bitter rivals, the hockey commonality forged an immediate bond. After a few minutes of conversation, Wayne asked, "Are you riding the Tour with anyone?"

I responded that I was riding solo and openly questioning that decision.

Shaking his head, he said, "Are you crazy?? It is too dangerous to do this race solo! I can't believe your wife let you get on the plane by yourself!"

I readily agreed with both assertions.

Just then, the French-Canadian father-son combo from breakfast joined us. Coincidentally, Wayne and the father were friends and the three of them had ridden together since Banff. I casually asked if I could tag along with them for the day and they said sure. Introductions and handshakes followed. Mario (the father) and Vincent (the son) were from Montreal, Canada and decided to race the Tour Divide a mere six weeks prior to the start. Vincent was 24 years old and Mario thought the Tour would be a great father-son bonding experience before Vincent immersed himself with career and family. Humorously, Vincent was the guy from Day 1 adorned with a box of pizza strapped to his back! I asked him how that went and he responded, "I've had better ideas!"

Incidentally, Mario, Wayne and I were all roughly the same age. In fact, I discovered that Wayne and I were born exactly two weeks apart.

We left the hotel at 10AM and made several lengthy stops for food, provisions and, most importantly, a large supply of electrolyte tablets. The process of filling stomachs, bottles and bags took over an hour. Clearly none of us was eager to leave Fernie. When we finally got our shit together just after 11AM and reached the outskirts of Fernie, a 600-car freight train crossed our route and further delayed our exit. Omen? 47 miles to Butts Cabin was sounding better and better.

The roads out of Fernie were wet, but in decent shape and we began to ascend approximately eight miles beyond the town limits. For the next four hours, we covered 20 mucky miles and gained several thousand feet of elevation. We ultimately crested at the Flathead Pass before enjoying a lengthy downhill. During the ride, we cheerily basked in the light rain and hail as well as the tropical 38-degree temperatures. (Apologies in advance as I tend to rely on sarcasm in place of actual humor. I also do not like Oxford commas or grammar Nazis who thumb their noses at split infinitives, but those are personal problems.) In addition to the alluring weather, a burning sensation arose in my left Achilles tendon that acutely worsened as the day progressed. Yep, my Tour Divide was going rather swimmingly.

A few miles below Flathead Pass, I pedaled around a curve and screeched to a halt. Wayne trailed by a short distance and likewise slid to a stop in response to my wildly waving outstretched arms.

"Brent, what's up?" asked Wayne.

I put my index finger to my lips and pointed down the road. Less than 200 yards away, a mama black bear and her two cubs played on the road. At least I assumed that the cubs were hers, though I guess theoretically she could have cubnapped them. Wayne and I sat still, mesmerized. The bears were too far away for a good picture (sorry Crazy Larry), but too close for comfort. The mama sensed our presence, looked up, and stared at us for a few seconds. I quickly recalled the warning that hell hath no fury like the wrath of a mama bear protecting her cubs from threat, real or perceived. I then remembered the second warning that an attacking bear can move REALLY fast.

I glanced sideways at Wayne and said, "Now what?"

Wayne just shrugged. On impulse, I grasped the whistle attached to a string around my neck, put it to my lips, and blew three sharp blasts. The bears looked toward us and snickered with derision. Actually, I just imagined that. Ten seconds passed and then the mama gathered her progeny and led them into the woods. We waited five minutes, during which time Mario and Vincent caught up to us. Then we all slowly coasted toward the spot where the bears disappeared before pedaling furiously for a few minutes until we felt safe.

I thought of an ancient Chinese proverb that asserts that a mountain biker does not have to ride faster than an attacking bear. He simply needs to ride faster than the slowest rider in the group! My apologies to Vincent who brought up the rear at that moment. Okay, that was a biker's tale and not an ancient proverb. My apologies to the creators of Chinese proverbs.

At a distance of 200 yards to the bears, we probably faced no imminent danger. Regardless, the experience starkly reminded us to take nothing lightly on the Tour Divide and to remain vigilant at all times.

It was nearly 4PM by the time we concluded our visit to the 'Dancing Bears' attraction at La Carnival de Tour Divide. Not only did we fail to win a stuffed animal, but we faced the prospect of getting wretchedly wet as the already dark and miserable skies were starting to look darker and more miserable. Sticking with the carnival motif, we were poised to enter nature's dunking booth. At 5:15PM we arrived at Butts Cabin, just as the sky burst forth with hoses, pitchforks and daggers.

Butts Cabin is a one-room shack no bigger than a typical American kid's bedroom. Inside were a table, an old spring bed and a couple bunks. I have no idea who "Butts" is or was, but it was immediately evident that only a limited number of butts could fit in such a tiny space. When we arrived, there were already four racers inhabiting the cabin, all of whom had already decided to stay the night. Fitting eight of us was going to be tight, but our options were limited as the next campground was 40 miles beyond Butts Cabin.

Mario gazed at the sky and remarked, "I don't like the prospect of venturing out in a storm and slogging 40 more miles in the mud." Vincent, Wayne and I echoed Mario's sentiments. We thus joined our new friends and hunkered down in Butts Cabin for the night. Being the pioneers that we were, each of us staked a claim to a section of the floor.

Once settled in the Cabin, our conversation turned to race-goals. I shared that my primary goal entailed finishing the race somehow and someway, no matter how long it took. The irony of this goal was rich considering that I had nearly thrown in the towel the day before. I was also painstakingly aware that the historical annual finish rate for the Tour Divide was approximately 45%. In other words, for every 100 racers who depart from Banff on the second Friday in June, only 45 reach the finish in Antelope

Wells. That finishing rate dropped below 30% for first-time Tour racers.

My secondary goals were time-oriented with an ambitious goal of a 27-day finish based on average mileage of 100 miles per day. The less ambitious goal consisted of a 30-day finish as 30 days was the unwritten deadline among Tour Divide aficionados that separated "racers" from "tourers." Wayne and Mario shared that their goals and mind-sets were nearly identical, namely to finish at all costs, but strive for under 30 days if possible.

We were off to a bad start. Advanced algebra confirmed this. Actually, simple math confirmed this. We had ridden just over 214 route miles in three days for an average of barely 70 miles per day. A 30-day finish required an average of nearly 95 miles per day from this point forward. Mario confidently asserted that improved weather, better terrain conditions, and adaption to the rigors of daily racing would put us on track. I was not as confident, but liked his positivity.

At 7PM, three more racers barged into Butts Cabin hoping to shack up for the night. Though space was limited, we rearranged the exquisite furniture and made room for them. For those performing neither advanced algebra, nor simple math, that took us to 11 guys crammed into a single-room cabin with every square foot of beds, floor and even table covered with cold, wet bodies.

Talking ceased and eleven sets of eyes closed at 9PM. Unfortunately, I failed to find the arms of Morpheus. A cacophony of snores, creaking bedsprings, creaking floorboards, and farts practically shook the cabin off its moorings. Combine those interior sounds with the outside sounds of wildlife, thunder and spattering rain on a metal roof, and the total audio package reminded me of the climax of the Beatles' song *A Day in the Life* (from the *Sergeant Pepper's* album) when 17 instruments are played at once, rising to a discordant crescendo. At least I luxuriated on a cold hard floor (there is that sarcasm again). For the 15th time in three days, I asked myself what the hell was I doing there?! Only this time, I posited the question in jest, as I knew exactly why I was there.

Flathead Valley Road

Butts Cabin

**Chapter 10 – "Red and white, blue suede shoes,
I'm Uncle Sam, how do you do?"
— Grateful Dead, *U.S. Blues***

Tour Divide Day 4 - 71 Miles - Butts Cabin, Flathead Valley, British Columbia to Eureka, Montana. When 11 guys cram into a small cabin for the night, it is inevitable that when the first guy gets up, everyone gets up. For some reason, the first guy was up at 4:45AM. Maybe the rancid air polluted by collective flatulence was finally too much for him. I was pretty much awake anyway because I pretty much did not sleep and I pretty much could not wait to get the hell out of there.

By 5:30AM, we were all packed and ready to go again. The skies had partially cleared and, while it was quite chilly, there was no imminent threat of rain. To energize the mood for the day, I cranked Christopher Cross's *Ride Like the Wind* on my Bluetooth speaker for the first of many times over the next 30 days. For those born after 1985 and not familiar with the song, the chorus goes, "Well I've got such a long way to go, to make it to the border of Mexico, so I'll ride like the wind, ride like the wind." I followed that up with Willie Nelson's *On the Road Again*. By then, not only did I want to leave, but everyone including the Butts Cabin concierge and front-desk staff also wanted me to leave. Thankfully, Wayne, Mario and Vincent were not quite ready to kick me off their island!

The first ten miles from the Cabin served up a nice 1300 foot climb to get the blood flowing and legs moving. We peaked in a tranquil clearing and then descended for roughly 15 miles on a soft rutted dirt road with stirring mountain views and deathly still forests. After the descent, we started slowly climbing again and wound our way on a double-track jeep trail that cut a quiet path between two towering parallel mountain ranges.

Then the fun began.

First, we missed a barely marked turn and had to retrace our track along the dreaded blue line. Then we rode a twisty-turny overgrown single-track trail alongside what we think was either the Columbia River, the Kootenay River or the Flathead River (did it really matter?) and across several deep muddy creeks. Finally, the trail abruptly ended at a wall. In Tour Divide lore (hereinafter "Tour Lore"), there are several spots along the route that have gained notoriety for either their hardship or their unique nature. After Koko Claims, this wall was the next big one.

It is hard to explain "The Wall" adequately. It is the gateway to a monster 2,000-foot climb, but the first few hundred feet monopolized our attention. I looked at the guys and queried, "How the hell are we going to get our bikes up this thing?" The character Vizzini from the classic movie *The Princess Bride* suddenly came to mind as scaling The Wall with our burly 50+ pound bikes seemed "absolutely, totally and in all other ways inconceivable." For starters, but for the red line on our Garmin computers, we would never have guessed that The Wall was even a trail. It had a 45% grade and looked like something formed by an angry mudslide. On the bright side, we knew from Tour Lore that it was only a quarter-mile long and that the best way to get up the infernal thing was to approach it like a chess match or puzzle, carefully plotting every move.

If someone created written instructions for scaling the wall, it would read like as follows:

First, put both hands on your grips and loosely grab the brakes with your fingers.

Second, thrust your bike forward and upward for a few feet and quickly lock your brakes.

Third, look down for a foothold for the right foot and one for the left foot and deposit feet in the footholds. If no footholds, look for a tree and use it as a butt-rest.

Fourth, once your feet and/or butt are secure, push the bike another two feet and repeat the foothold/buttrest search.

Fifth, repeat two or three more times, then stop and catch your breath. If it helps, feel free to mutter profanity.

Sixth, repeat, repeat, repeat, repeat. Whatever you do, do not slip because if you fall to your left, you will fall 50 to 100 feet down a steep ravine and, if you do not break your neck from the fall, you will have to circle back around to the base and start all over again.

This ain't no hokey pokey, but that's what it's all about.

Fortunately, for us, the conditions were not too bad and we successfully scaled The Wall in under 10 minutes. I cannot imagine how people make it up The Wall in the pouring rain and I do not see how anyone with poor upper body strength can make it up. Anyway, I felt that we admirably conquered The Wall.

After The Wall, we continued to climb and climb and climb, with the knowledge and anticipation that upon reaching the summit of the ascent, we would enjoy nothing but miles of downhill all the way to the US border. And oh what a downhill it was. Steep. Fast. Rocky. FUN!!

This downhill also displayed the glaring disparity in mountain-biking skills between me, on one hand, and Wayne, Mario and Vincent, on the other. Those three were strong dudes and great riders. In fact, Wayne and Mario were accomplished ironman triathletes and Wayne had competed in a cross-country road-bike race called TransAmerica. Actually, "strong triathletes" is an understatement. These guys compete in "DECA" ironman triathlons. I had never heard of the concept, but a DECA is where you do a full ironman triathlon every day for ten straight days. WTF? That is batshit crazy territory. Anyway, this would be the first of many technical sections in the coming days where I raced ahead, waited for them, and then repeated the process several times before reaching the bottom.

This descent was the first time I weighed the benefit of comradeship with the detriment of time sacrifice. Based on my Day 2 misadventures, the scales tilted heavily toward comradeship. Sticking with Mario, Vincent and Wayne would simply require a little patience when the route turned technical. I was okay with that. These were good guys and I was cognizant that my odds of success were greater with them than without. As consideration for their letting me interlope with their small group, I aimed to repay them by helping them improve their mountain biking skills.

The only other negative with the descent was that every rocky jolt sent a sharp pain into my left Achilles tendon. By the time we reached the bottom of the descent, I could barely put pressure on my left pedal. However, by then we were only 3 miles of smooth pavement to the US border in Roosville, Montana and the excitement of entering the US masked the pain. After taking a few mandatory pictures in front of the "Welcome to the United States of America" sign, which oddly was erected on the Canada side of the border, we rolled up to the customs window, answered a few mundane questions and were sent on our way.

On the other side of the border, I looked at Wayne and joked, "We have finally made it to the last country of the Tour Divide!"

"That's right," Wayne, responded with a wide grin, "it's all downhill from here!"

From the border, we enjoyed an easy rolling 10-mile pavement ride to the town of Eureka, Montana, arriving just as the sun was setting over the western hills. In Eureka, we checked into a cheap roadside motel and wolfed down juicy cheeseburgers at a greasy spoon across the street from the motel.

Meanwhile, by the time we dismounted from the bikes, my Achilles tendon hurt so badly that I could hardly walk. This was distressing after fighting so hard to turn the mental corner. I called Lisa and expressed serious concern that the sore Achilles might end my race. She advised me to try to reach my good friend and podiatrist Gary Feldman and get his distant diagnosis.

I called Gary after dinner and he recommended ice, KT tape, Advil three times a day, and testing different positions with my seat and shoe cleats. I asked whether I was risking a complete tear by continuing to ride and Gary assured me that a tear was unlikely. He said that my ability to continue riding was solely and simply dependent upon how much pain I was willing to tolerate.

Wonderful.

There was nothing left to do but go to sleep and hope for the best in the morning. I hoped Wayne was not a snorer.

Mario and Vincent

Damn it's pretty out here!

Insert name of river

Base of the Wall

Top of The Wall

Entering the last country of the race! LOL

Chapter 11 – "Video killed the radio star, video killed the radio star" — The Buggles, *Radio Star*

Prior to the Tour Divide, when friends and family asked what the race would be like, I often responded with terms like "wilderness" and "off the grid" and "disconnected" and "radio silence." Truth be told, while I successfully maintained a news and career blackout during the Tour, I did not fully detach from civilization as I armed myself with an array of technology serving many purposes, several of which are bound to elicit scoffs from bikepacking purists. To each his/her own.

What follows is a summary description of my various devices. For those of you planning a bikepacking or similar outdoor adventure, you will find this information pertinent and interesting. For those of you just 'along for the ride' (pun intended) and who do not care about technical details, feel free to skip ahead to the next chapter.

The most important device was the Garmin eTrex 30 bike computer that I used for navigation. A week before the race, all racers received via email an up-to-date GPS data file of the entire 2018 Tour Divide route. After downloading this file to my eTrex, I could zoom out and see the entire 2700+ mile route on the screen or I could zoom in to within 100 yards of the triangle representing me. As mentioned in prior chapters, the red line on the eTrex served as both my lifeline and my compass. My inexperience with the device frustrated me the first few days of the Tour, but I finally had everything dialed in by Day 5. After that, it was smooth navigational sailing except for the occasional missed turn.

Speaking of missed turns, there were usually two reasons for missing a turn. The first resulted from not paying attention and not looking down at the eTrex and thus not seeing the off-route blue line until too late. The second was due to parallel paths. To illustrate, picture arriving at a fork in the trail with two paths diverging but appearing to run parallel beyond your line of vision. Regardless of which trail you select, the triangle still appears on the red line until the trails distinctly separate. When lucky, the trail separation occurs within a few hundred yards. When unlucky, trails run closely parallel for a few miles. Most often, we either noticed clear tire-tracks in the dirt or won the coin-flip and chose correctly. However, there were several occasions where we suffered the scourge of the dreaded blue line and had to backtrack.

Of all of my devices, the eTrex was the easiest to manage because it ran on two AA batteries that consistently lasted two full days. I carried a six-day supply of AA batteries at all times just to be safe.

The second most important device was a Garmin inReach SE+. The general web-surfing public followed the progress of Tour Divide racers on a website called Trackleaders.com thanks to SPOT GPS technology. Most racers rent a SPOT-tracker device that offers two basic functions: tracking and emergency exit. As long as the device is on, then a racer's location as well as other data is relayed from the SPOT-tracker at ten-minute intervals to the Trackleaders website. As for the emergency button, a racer must think long and hard about pressing that button, as it triggers an emergency rescue that could cost upwards of $25,000 depending on location and ease of exit.

An alternative to renting a SPOT-tracker is purchasing a Garmin inReach satellite communication device. In addition to tracking and emergency applications, the inReach pairs with an iPhone to provide unlimited texting, even when the iPhone is out of cell service range. This gave me the ability to communicate at all times with Lisa (one of her pre-conditions for my doing the race), and also allowed me to better manage an emergency if one arose. For example, if I had a catastrophic bike issue and needed rescue, I could let Lisa or the proper authorities know that I was not in physical danger and did not need an extraction with emergency personnel. The inReach was charged via USB and held an average charge of two to three days.

After navigation and communication, the next most important device (for me anyway) was my JBL Bluetooth speaker. I love music. I have to have music. In fact, later in this book is a whole chapter devoted to music. For safety and social reasons, I did not want to be tuned out with headphones. With Bluetooth technology, I could play Spotify and iTunes playlists on the speaker directly from my iPhone. The JBL was indestructible, waterproof, sufficiently loud, and had a clip that easily attached to my handlebar bag. As long as I did not blast the sound at full volume, it lasted between 10-12 hours on a single charge.

Next came the iPhone. Although I only had service for about 20% of the ride, I constantly used the iPhone for multiple functions. As mentioned above, I used it for text communication through an app that paired with my inReach. I took all of my pictures and videos on the iPhone — the videos are available on YOUTUBE if you search "Brent Goldstein's Tour Divide." At rest stops each day, I used the Notes app to jot down reminders of things that I saw or thought and then revisited the Notes app every night before going to sleep to type up a narrative of the day's events. I then cut and paste those notes into a Facebook post the next morning or the next time phone service was available. I used the weather app religiously (again, when in range) to check radar maps and high and low temperatures for the coming days. I used the internet app to check other racer progress and proximity on Trackleaders and I often checked my First Descents' fundraising page to see what donations arrived and to read the uplifting donor comments. I used Yelp to locate restaurants, hotels or specific retail needs in various towns as well as to determine opening and closing times for those establishments. Finally, I used the Facebook app as my social lifeline to the world outside, though admittedly my time on Facebook was limited to posting my daily updates, reading my friends' comments to the updates and occasionally responding to those comments. Speaking of friends' comments, I cannot understate how much daily affirmation I got from those comments. I will not be so overdramatic as to say they were life saving, but they were definitely essential in keeping me positive, motivated and, in some cases, inspired. With so many people following my journey via Facebook, failure was simply not an option.

Although the Garmin eTrex recorded all of the relevant data I could possibly need, I also used a Garmin Edge 820 bike computer for data viewing and uploading each day's ride to Strava[2]. The eTrex was clumsy when switching screens and, frankly, with all of the possibilities for missed turns, I never wanted to turn off the navigation screen. I have used the Edge 820 for data for the last five years and familiarity breeds comfort. I mounted the Edge right next to the eTrex and set the Edge to scroll between two screens. The first screen showed elapsed ride time for the day, current speed, total distance for the day, time of day, and current temperature. The second screen showed current elevation, total elevation gained for the day, ground gradient, and average speed. I did not look at all of these categories all of the time, but each one was important at certain times. For example, I constantly looked at gradient on a climb to gauge whether my legs were screaming at me because of weariness or because of steepness. Any grade of 10% or more on a 58-pound bike HURT and I could justify scaling back the effort. Anything over 14% meant get off and walk, as cranking the pedals was not worth the effort. Whereas, if I was hurting on a 3%-4% grade, I knew I was tired and should probably take a break.

Finally, for night riding and camping, I used a kLite Bikepacker Pro Dynamo light mounted on my handlebars and a Petzl Actik Core headlight

---

2   *"Strava is a social fitness network that is used to track cycling, running, and swimming activities, among others, using GPS data. Activities are recorded via the Strava mobile application or GPS-enabled fitness watches or cycling computers. Users can upload activities to the Strava site directly, via the Strava mobile application, or via one of Strava's data partners such as Garmin. The software provides statistics such as distance, pace, speed and elevation, and provides comparisons with other users' activities."* — Wikipedia

that attached to a headband.

The next obvious question is how did I keep all this stuff charged? Despite all of my rookie foibles, I am proud of my success in managing the logistics of device charging. One of my most important early decisions was to install a Schmidt Son Dynamo Hub in my front wheel axle. The Dynamo hub garners power from the rotation of the wheel and sends a charge to a switch on the handlebars. From the switch, there are two wires. The first wire connects directly to the kLite handlebar light and the second connects to a Sinewave Revolution cache. The cache is a device the size of a small television remote that converts the hub-generated electric charge to USB output. As I only used the light at night and did not do significant after-dark riding, I primarily kept the switch aimed at the cache with the iPhone being the main recipient of the cache charge. Although the phone was mostly in airplane mode throughout the Tour, the Bluetooth music output combined with the Garmin inReach function rapidly drained my iPhone battery. Accordingly, as long as I kept the iPhone sufficiently charged, I could rotate the other devices with the cache as needed.

The only problem with the cache is that it provided a slow charge and was limited to charging one device at a time. As I knew there would be multi-day stretches on the Tour where electricity was inaccessible, I also brought an Anker 13000 mAh PowerCore rechargeable battery that held enough power to generate eight to ten full device charges. Finally, I also carried two dual-USB plug-in wall chargers so that I could charge four devices at once any time I was in a motel, with re-charging the Anker always being the top priority. It was a constant juggling act keeping everything charged (and keeping track!), but I had the system working seamlessly by the end of the first week of the Tour.

Tour Divide electronics

Chapter 12 – "Little darling, it's been a long cold lonely winter
Little darling, it feels like years since it's been here
Here comes the sun, Here comes the sun,
and I say It's all right"
— The Beatles, *Here Comes the Sun*

Tour Divide Day 5 - 92 Miles - Eureka, MT to Whitefish, MT. My Achilles still hurt like hell when we rolled from the motel the morning of Day 5. Following doctor's orders, I wrapped my foot and ankle with KT tape, swallowed three Advil, stretched the calf and Achilles tendon areas, and decided to start pedaling and wish the pain away. After spending an inordinate amount of time grabbing provisions at a local grocery store, we were on our way at 9AM.

It was a cool but blissfully sunny morning and the first ten miles consisted of easy rolling pavement south from Eureka. I managed the Achilles pain by lowering my seat a half inch and by unclipping my left foot from the left pedal. This allowed my foot to move forward and use my heel as the contact point with the pedal (thus reducing the flex of the ankle). I lost pedaling efficiency from being unclipped, but *c'est la vie*. Funny side note: we rode the pavement section between 9AM and 10AM on Tuesday, June 12 at the same time that the Washington Capitals were holding their Stanley Cup victory parade in D.C.. Since I still had phone service on the pavement, I propped my iPhone on my handlebars and watched a chunk of the parade via live simulcast, much to the amusement of my riding cohorts.

We eventually turned left from the paved road and began heading east on a dirt road. A mile down the dirt road, we stopped for a quick snack break and a partial disrobing as the air was warming. Across the road from where we stopped was a little farmhouse adorned with an excessive number of "Jesus Saves", "Trump 2016" and "Don't Mess With My Guns" signs. We found this particularly amusing considering the remoteness of this country dirt road. I am sure that the number of fingers on my left hand exceeded the number of cars that passed this house each day.

While admiring the passionate signage, a little old woman came out of the house and asked where we were from and where we were going. We told her about the race, she asked a few more questions, she started to ramble on, I started to daydream, fell asleep with my eyes open, and then I woke up as she blessed us in the name of the father, son and Holy Ghost. I immediately thought of the golf-shop scene in the movie *Caddyshack* when Rodney Dangerfield is buying a bunch of crap for his Asian guest when he looks at the guest and says, "I think this place is restricted, Wang, so don't tell 'em you're Jewish!"

I opted not to tell our new friend that my last name was Goldstein.

Finally, she asked, "Why the hell don't you boys have guns if you're going into bear country?"

We pointed to our cans of bear-spray and she said, "Well, I guess that'll do. But be careful now, ya hear?"

We nodded and she waddled back into her house, presumably to light prayer candles and say a few Hail Mary's for us. We each gave one another one of those "did that just happen" looks and then burst out laughing.

After leaving our new right-wing patron saint, we entered the Flathead National Forest and enjoyed a glorious climb up and over Whitefish Pass on a moderate-grade rocky dirt road. The views at the top of the pass were nothing special, but that changed in a hurry as the route swung down and around a bend and introduced us to the jagged west wall of Glacier National Park some 20 to 30 miles in the distance. The stark beauty of the gray snow-capped mountains steeply rising over the distant green valley left me breathless.

We continued dropping through a thick forest that gave way to a stretch of sparse pines that appeared to be the victims of an old forest fire. Between the charred trees and the distant looming wall of Glacier National Park, the surrounding terrain took on an otherworldly appearance.

At the bottom of the descent, the road turned south and crossed a bridge over a raging creek. We stopped on the bridge to eat lunch and take pictures. During one picture, I must have posed too provocatively (showing too much leg maybe?) as Wayne got distracted and dropped my phone, cracking my screen. I planned to replace the phone after the Tour anyway, so no big deal. Anyway, the only reason this stop is even worth mentioning (besides the cracked screen) is that the view down the creek toward Glacier Park provided one of the most dramatic photos of the Tour.

Following lunch, we rode for an hour on a stretch of chillaxed pavement before turning off for a 15-ish mile climb to Red Meadow Pass. Back at Butts Cabin, a fellow cabin-dweller named Ron told us that he had ridden Red Meadow Pass three weeks prior to the race and that two feet of snow covered a five to ten mile swath before and after the pass. The region had significantly warmed and dried since then, so we began the ascent hoping that most of the snow had melted.

As we advanced toward the summit and each mile ticked by without snow, we felt luckier and luckier. Finally, a half mile from the pass, the pavement abruptly turned from black to white. We had reached the snow. Fortunately, earlier riders packed down the snow, not well enough to ride over or through, but well enough that the push on foot was not bad. After ten minutes of hiking, we reached the summit of Red Meadow Pass and were enraptured by a pristine mountain lake sprouting a precipitous rock wall above the far shore. Although the sun sat low in the afternoon western sky and our goal for the day was to reach the town of Whitefish, Montana by evening, the serenity of the lake was so entrancing that we stopped for pictures and a food break.

After the lake, we faced another half mile of snow hiking before earning the reward of a ripping 30-mile descent on a gravel road piercing a long stretch of thick forest before depositing us at sunset alongside the eastern bank of the placid six-mile long Whitefish Lake. Early evening was a special time to ride along the lake. Between the still air and absence of sun-glare, the smooth water surface provided us with a crystal-clear reflection of the mountains that soared over the western edge of the lake.

From the end of Whitefish Lake, we pedaled another few miles to the outskirts of Whitefish, first stopping at a roadside carwash to spray the mud off our bikes, and then finding a charming little motel in the center of town called the Downtowner Inn. Okay, maybe charming is too complimentary, but the Downtowner Inn did provide the number one Tour Divide amenity besides a warm bed — a washer/dryer!

We threw our bikes in our rooms and our clothes in the washer and then enjoyed a hot meal with a few other Tour racers at a local Mexican restaurant before excitedly returning to the motel for a good night's sleep. My Achilles tendon was no less sore in Whitefish than when I dismounted in Eureka the day before, but I rode 92 miles over two mountain passes without major issue and felt cautiously optimistic that I could continue dealing with and managing the pain.

Whitefish Pass flow

Views going up Whitefish Pass

Bottom of Whitefish Pass descent

Mario descending from Whitefish Pass

West Glacier Nat'l Park

Red Meadow Pass

Red Meadow Pass Lake

Chapter 13 – "Take a little trip, take a little trip and see Take a little trip, take a little trip with me"
— War, *Low Rider*

Tour Divide Day 6 - 85 miles - Whitefish, MT to Flathead National Forest, MT. Quality bike-shops are in short supply along the Tour Divide route. In fact, bike shops are in short supply along the route. If your bike needs service, major or minor, and a shop is nearby, you are playing with fire if you elect to wait until the next town with a shop, as it could be hundreds of miles away. I had two broken spokes on my rear tire that needed replacement. I was also experiencing numbness in the fingertips of my left hand and wanted to switch my grips to thick grips known as Ergons. Finally, I needed to find some relief, any relief, for my inflamed left Achilles tendon and determined that swapping my clipless pedals for platform pedals would be my best option.[3] Additionally, Mario wanted new tires and Wayne needed a new chain.

Whitefish was the last town with a bike shop until Helena, which was over two hundred miles away. While an early start would have been ideal, the shop did not open until 9AM. Fortuitously, the later start allowed me to meet my friend (and Whitefish native) Chuck Ludden for breakfast. It was great to see a friendly face. It was even better that Chuck brought me prescription pain-relievers from his orthopedic medic friend. My Achilles tendon thanked him profusely. I am not certain, but accepting medication from Chuck may have constituted my second rules violation of the Tour. Whatever.

After breakfast, I rejoined the boys at the hotel for checkout and then we all headed over to Glacier Cyclery for repairs. The guys in the bike shop immediately dropped everything to help us and could not have been

---

[3] *For those unfamiliar with bike pedal choices, here is a good explanation from a blog on www.purecycles.com of the difference between toe-clips, clipless pedals and platform pedals: "Toe-clips mount to the front of the pedal and work with straps to lock-in the rider's foot so they can generate power on the "upstroke" by pulling up as the pedals go around. The straps really do more of the securing than the toe-clips, but the clips keep the straps open so you can easily slide a foot in and, because they grab your foot and the pedal in that binder-clip-y way of theirs, the name toe-clips stuck. So what do you call pedals that do away with the need for a metal toe-clip dangling off the front of your pedal? That's right, clipless. The first clipless pedals were actually manufactured by ski-binding maker Look, and they're still cranking 'em out today. Given the popularity of toe-clips at the time, they needed some way to differentiate and so the term "clipless" was born. And that make sense. You don't really clip into clipless pedals anyway. Maybe you click into them, maybe you lock in, but it's not a clip. The toe-clip is gone from the pedal and all that remains is a small catch to receive the cleat on your shoe. Platform pedals contain neither toe-clips, nor a cleat-locking mechanism. Your shoe simply rides loose on the pedal platform."*

friendlier or more accommodative. The various repairs took two hours, during which time we ransacked (metaphorically of course) the local grocery store and restocked our food supplies. We hit the road at 11AM.

Nothing particularly special or memorable stuck out about the first 40 miles from Whitefish. The terrain was primarily pavement through flat to lightly rolling farm country. The most noteworthy occurrence during that stretch involved a sketchy-looking guy on an old 10-speed bike approaching us on the edge of Whitefish and asking with a wink, "You guys need anything to make your ride more fun?"

I was initially confused, but as comprehension dawned, I responded, "No man, but thanks for the offer."

As we pedaled away, Mario wondered aloud what the guy could have possibly possessed that would make our ride more fun. I smiled and responded, "Drugs Mario. Drugs. We can go back if you like?"

Vincent looked at his dad with a grin and we all laughed.

The second most noteworthy moment leaving Whitefish occurred several miles out of town with Wayne snapping his brand new chain after a sudden gearshift. Not wanting to risk further chain issues, Wayne immediately flagged down a passing pick-up truck and caught a ride back to Glacier Cyclery in Whitefish to have it replaced again. It happened so fast, that we did not even have the chance to ask Wayne whether we should wait at that spot for him or slowly carry on and hook up later in the day. Mario, Vincent and I chose the latter and pressed forward with a stop at a grocery in Columbia Falls at mile ten for some medical supplies (as Vincent's Achilles tendon was bothering him and I was feeling new soreness in my other Achilles tendon). From Columbia Falls, we 'slow-pedaled' the next 30 miles until Wayne caught us.

At mile 40, we entered the Swan River National Refuge and tackled a bug-infested dirt climb that rose 1700 feet over seven miles followed by a fast gravel descent alongside a stream where we refilled our water. While stopped, two recognizable bikers pulled up. They were a friendly duo I nicknamed "Bro-Dude and the Kid." Bro-Dude was from Austin, Texas and the Kid was from somewhere in Minnesota. Bro-Dude said that he was riding the great divide route for the third time but was quick to point out that, "I'm not racing, duuuuude. I'm just chillin'!" The Kid grinned and nodded in agreement. We originally met them briefly in Eureka and then again at the bike shop in Whitefish. Both of them started in Banff with the Grand Depart, but they wisely skipped Koko Claims.

When I asked Bro-Dude why he skipped Koko Claims, he simply said, "Duuuuuude, why would anyone want to ride that nasty shit?" That was the smartest thing anyone had said to me in days. After a few more minutes of small talk, Bro-Dude and the Kid waved hearty goodbyes, smiled and said, "See y'all down the trail, duuuudes" and took off.

After our encounter with the happy-go-lucky boys of summer, we rolled forward on a wooded service road as afternoon turned to evening. There was a short climb at mile 60 followed by a final upward push from mile 67 through 80 that crested on a small plateau that gave us front row (bike) seats to a magnificent gloaming view of a snow-capped mountain ridge on the opposite side of the valley beneath us.

We finished the day with an eerie five-mile descent into the darkness. At 10:15PM, the road leveled next to an open clearing in the forest. We briefly contemplated pressing forward for another hour behind the beams of our lamplights. However, Mario correctly pointed out that there had been few appealing camping spots over the past 15 miles and suggested stopping for the night. Nobody objected. I was glad someone was paying attention.

This was the sixth night of the Tour, but my first spent in a tent. I was both excited and nervous. Over a month had passed since my camping "test-drive" at home and I had forgotten how to erect the damn tent! I ultimately figured it out, but it took a laughable amount of time. I finally pounded the last tent stake in the ground only to look up and see Wayne, Mario and Vincent grinning at my ineptitude.

With playtime over, Vincent walked over and asked me to give him all of my food. I jokingly asked, "Is this a hold-up?"

Vincent responded, "No you silly jackass, we are deep in grizzly country. We have to combine all of the food in a bear-proof bag and hang it on the other side of the clearing." Vincent did not actually call me a jackass. He was far too polite and did not know me well enough to confirm that I really am a jackass. I am sure he was thinking it though!

With the food safely stowed, it was time for sleep. I crawled into my tent, zipped up the front, and slid snugly into my sleeping quilt. As my eyelids grew heavy, I quietly reflected. Overall, it had been an easy and pleasant day. Other than a brief sprinkle in Columbia Falls and a ho-hum first 40 miles, we enjoyed partly sunny skies and comfortable temperatures all day. I was satisfied with our 85-mile effort, especially considering our various delays departing Whitefish.

After 6 days of riding, my legs felt strong and I finally felt like I had adapted to the rhythms of the Tour. Best of all, I was starting to really enjoy the experience despite the punishing first few days and the nagging Achilles tendon (which still had not improved). I briefly questioned whether I was diminishing the adventure by not venturing forth solo, but I really liked Wayne, Mario and Vincent, our riding speeds and endurance were compatible, and I believed and determined that my odds of successfully completing the race were far greater in their company, at least in the short-term.

My last thoughts before falling into a deep sleep were of Lisa and my girls. I missed them. I hoped they were proud of me. I knew the girls would crack up picturing their dad in a tent.

Sunset over the mountains

Sunset with camera filter

Chapter 14 – "Movin' to Montana soon,
         Gonna be a Dental Floss tycoon (yes I am)
         Movin' to Montana soon
         Gonna be a mennil-toss flykune"
         — Frank Zappa, *Montana*

Tour Divide Day 7 - 87 miles - Flathead National Forest, Montana to Ovando, Montana. I survived my first Tour night in a tent. In fact, I slept quite soundly despite a steady rain that fell through the night. Fortunately, the rain cleared out before dawn and the morning greeted us with wet gear, refreshingly cool (but not cold) temperatures, and the first hints of sunshine. We retrieved the bear-bag and were pleased that no thieves made off with our food during the night. Maybe the local bears had more discriminating palates than we had! After eating and packing up, we rolled from the campsite at 8AM, starting with a short climb followed by 30 miles of rolling dirt and gravel roads culminating with our arrival at the Holland Lake Lodge, a rustic resort on an idyllic lake called . . . drumroll . . . Holland Lake.

As we walked into the lodge, the first sound we heard was, "Duuuuuuuudes, you finally made it!"

Sitting at a table against the back window with shit-eating grins were none other than Bro-Dude and the Kid. Bro-Dude said that they did not arrive at the lodge until well after midnight the night before and then stated, "We just couldn't get our mojo working for an early departure, so we've just been chillin' this morning."

The Kid nodded in agreement before sagely adding, "You gotta try the cheeseburgers!"

Although it was still morning, it had been over three hours since our paltry campsite breakfast, so we took the Kid's advice and feasted on giant cheeseburgers with heaping sides of fries and chocolate chip cookies. We probably loitered longer than we should (this was becoming a pattern), but the confines of the Lodge were so warm and inviting, and the view of the lake so serene that it was hard to rush back out. Plus, we enjoyed the entertaining company of Bro-Dude and the Kid.

From the Lodge, we faced 18 miles and 2,500+ feet of ascent to the snow-covered Richmond Pass in the Lewis and Clark National Forest. The climb was strenuous and the final push up and over the pass involved a snowy hike-a-bike very similar to the snow-hike over Red Meadow Pass two days before. The only difference, and it was a big one, was a scary section where we traversed an awkward 45-degree side hill angle.

Overcoming gravity necessitated our forcefully planting our feet in the snow to keep from falling over and sliding hundreds of feet downhill to potentially gruesome outcomes.

Once through the snow, we had a joyously fast and scenic 12-mile descent ending near a resupply area featured in the *Ride the Divide* documentary called Seeley Lake. A visit to Seeley Lake would have been nice, but it was two miles off the route and we only had 27 miles to the town of Ovando, our planned stopping point for the day. We therefore bypassed Seeley Lake, continued through a couple more small climbs at the 60-mile and 70-mile marks, and then bombed another super-fast descent (where Mario suffered a flat tire) that took us into Ovando, arriving at 8PM.

Ovando is a small three-street town (Main Street, Birch Street and Pine Street) with a population of 50, an inn, a covered wagon, a giant tipi, an old jail that doubles as a bunkhouse, a fly-fishing store and two restaurants. I mention the tipi as Bro-Dude and the Kid arrived in Ovando shortly before us and took up residence in the tipi. They yelled out friendly "whattup duuuuuudes" when we rolled into town. I really liked those guys!

We checked into a quaint country farmhouse called the Ovando Inn and were welcomed warmly by the owners, LeeAnn and Fred. In fact, LeeAnn and Fred tracked us on the Trackleaders.com website and stayed open for an extra hour just to await our arrival. Anticipating our hunger, LeeAnn graciously placed a call up to Trixi's Antler Saloon and persuaded them to keep their kitchen open to serve us a late dinner.

Trixi's sat atop a hill overlooking Ovando and was a classic "down-home" country bar. The waitress was very sweet, but I got nothing but blank stares TWICE when I used lines from the movie *Fletch*. First, when she took my order, I said, "I'll have a Bloody Mary and a steak sandwich . . . and a steak sandwich."

No reaction. So I ordered a beer and a Bison Burger . . . and a Bison Burger.

Then when it was time to pay up, I said, "Just put it on the Underhill's bill."

Again, nothing. Total pop-culture strikeout. Regardless, we could not have asked for better hospitality than we received from everyone in Ovando.

Good morning Day 7!

Holland Lake

Holland Lake Lodge

Richmond Pass descent

Snowy Richmond Peak

Chapter 15 –   "I am Superman and I know what's happening,
I am Superman and I can do anything"
— R.E.M., *Superman*

Tour Divide Day 8 - 102 miles from Ovando, MT to Helena, MT. Part two of the dining experience in Ovando consisted of a gargantuan 7AM breakfast at the Stray Bullet Cafe. Our bodies required a caloric pigfest as we intended to make an ambitious 102-mile push for Helena, the state capital of Montana. Mileage-wise, this would be our longest day so far. Additionally, we faced a massive day of ascending with four climbs totaling over 8,000 cumulative feet. After breakfast, we packed our belongings at the Inn, bid adieu to LeeAnn and Fred, and mounted our two-wheeled steeds. As we pulled out, we also waved so long to Bro-Dude and the Kid who were casually reclining in front of their Tipi sipping coffees without a care in the world.

"Duuuuudes, have an awesome ride today!" shouted Bro-Dude as we slowly rode off. Sadly, we never saw those characters again.

The morning ride kicked off with a mellow ten miles of fast and flat dirt road under a glorious rising sun. From a distance, the dirt road appeared to head smack into the base of an impenetrable mountain range. However, as we drew within a few miles of the range, rising individual mountain flanks became discernible and a fissure between two flanks appeared.

A mile before reaching the range, Wayne let out a sudden loud "whoop" after reading a message on his phone. I looked at him and said, "You just saved 15% by calling Geico, didn't you?"

"Even better," he responded. "I just got word from my business partner that a huge deal that was in the works before I left for the Tour just closed this morning and we earned a hefty fee! Boys, dinner on me tonight!"

I quickly turned to Mario and Vincent and said, "When we get to the next town later this morning, we need to Google the most expensive steakhouse in Helena!"

They both heartily and hungrily agreed.

Wayne just smiled.

A mile later, we reached the opening in the range and discovered a dirt road that pitched skyward into the belly of the range. It was quite the illusion. This first climb of the day returned us into the same Lewis and Clark National Forest where we climbed Richmond Pass the day before. The climb consisted of a moderate-grade 1800-foot ascent to a summit known as Huckleberry Pass. When I heard the name of the pass at breakfast that morning, I enjoyed a brief chuckle as I thought of Huckleberry Finn,

Huckleberry Hound and Frank Sinatra's Huckleberry Friend in the song *Moon River*.

Clearly energized by his successful business deal, Wayne raced up the climb ahead of us and was the first Huckleberry to reach the top. Once over the top, we flew down an eight-mile descent, arriving in the town of Lincoln, MT at noon.

Entering Lincoln, we immediately spotted a restaurant called the Scapegoat Eatery. What specifically grabbed our attention was a "Welcome Tour Dividers" sign and an inviting sun deck. On the Tour Divide, when you hit a quadfecta of food, sun, sun deck and a warm welcome, you stop! As we settled on the sun deck, the restaurant owner cheerily greeted us and shared that her son was also racing the Tour Divide. After asking where we each called home, she took our orders and pointed to a garden hose for rinsing off our bikes. She also directed our attention to a small canopy tent in the back yard of the restaurant that contained a table full of chocolate-chip cookies and other desserts that were *gratis* for Tour Divide racers.

We spent a leisurely hour and a half at the Scapegoat basking in the sun, filling our bellies, talking with a few locals, and bathing our bikes. Throwing a nod to one of my favorite movies of all-time, *Chitty Chitty Bang Bang*, the chocolate chip cookies were truly scrumptious.

After Lincoln, we still faced 60 miles and three Continental Divide crossings on the way to Helena. First up was a 2200-foot climb to either Stemple Pass or Granite Butte (the map was not clear about the correct name). The climb started moderately on a double-track jeep road that passed through a narrow valley dotted with old farmhouses and rusty farm equipment. We took a right past the last farmhouse and the trail immediately turned steep and rocky and got steeper and rockier the higher we climbed. A canopy of thick trees and overhanging branches enveloped the trail. We continued rising through a wondrous tunnel of nature. The surrounding woods were so dense in some spots that we could have ridden within mere feet of a lounging family of bears and not seen them. It was surreal.

Wayne and I left Mario and Vincent behind early on the climb. Even with grades exceeding 15%, we surprisingly "cleaned" the entire climb (in mountain bike lingo, to clean a climb means to ride the whole damn thing without putting a foot down on the ground). Mario and Vincent chose to save energy and walk the steepest sections of the climb and arrived at the top ten minutes after us. Thanks to the challenging but rideable terrain, the perfect weather, and the raw nature that encapsulated us, this was one of my favorite and most memorable climbs of the entire Tour.

From the summit of the climb, we reveled in a swift and steep descent that dumped us out into a picturesque green valley resembling a set from the movie *The Sound of Music*. We were moving so quickly toward the bottom of the descent that we apparently blew right past a farmhouse supposedly well known for providing food and shelter for Tour Divide racers and recreational riders on the Divide route. The owners of the farmhouse were either surprised or put-off that we did not stop as three miles later, we were overtaken by a man and woman in a black pick-up truck. We stopped and they pulled up next to us. The woman in the passenger seat rolled down her window and remarked, "You boys flew down that hill so fast that you missed the entrance of our farmhouse."

We responded with puzzled looks.

She continued, "Why don't you come back with us and grab some food and rest. If ya'll want, you can stay the night."

This was weird. We exchanged uncomfortable looks, thanked them and respectfully declined their offer. Wayne explained to them that it was 4:30PM, we had plenty of supplies, it was still 40 miles to Helena, and we wanted to get there at a reasonable hour. They seemed disappointed by our rejection and slowly turned around and returned to their farmhouse. I guess it was nice of them to chase us down, but it was a bizarre exchange.

Approaching the third major climb of the day, our sunny skies turned ominous and we prepared to get wet. Luckily, the clouds were all bark with no bite and we remained dry during the entire ascent. The climb started on a wide gravel road cutting a swath through lush green meadows. It then narrowed into a rocky Jeep trail that rose steeply into a thick and darkening forest. After 1800-feet of elevation gain, the trail crested at an unnamed pass that invisibly (as it was not marked) crossed the Continental Divide.

After a relatively short descent into a desolate, yet beautiful treeless valley, we faced one last climb up to a spookily stunning Priest Pass and our third crossing of the Divide that afternoon. I say spookily stunning because of a visual blending of barren landscape, eerie sunset, iridescent clouds, and mountaintop views that adjectives cannot adequately describe.

The day ended with a hair-raising rocky descent in the fading light that tested all of our ocular skills as well as our guts and, arguably, our intelligence. Once again, I had a distinct advantage over the others as I had ridden hundreds of descents like this over the years and had no fear navigating through rocks and irregularities in the road surface, even in poor light. There was no point in my riding down in front of the group and then waiting at the bottom of the descent. I therefore gave the three of them a five-minute head-start at the top, caught them a third of the way down, and repeated the process a couple more times until we reached the highway that led us the last 8 miles into Helena (at a relentless pace thanks to Mario leading the paceline).

Once in Helena, we checked into a complete and utter dump known as the Budget Inn Express (more on that in the next chapter), located just a few blocks off the Tour Divide route. With a 10PM arrival, Wayne dodged a monetary bullet, as there were no steakhouses open . . . or any other restaurants for that matter. Lamentably, our big celebratory dinner on Wayne consisted of a few Domino's pizzas and frosted cinnamon breadsticks.

Tour Divide veterans spin a tale that riders feel the most fatigue between days five through seven and then break through the metaphorical physical wall feeling like Superman. Sure enough, that happened to me between Ovando and Helena. I felt strong the entire day and was not even that spent after 102 otherwise grueling miles that, at any other time of year, would have immobilized me for three days. In fact, I felt my strongest on the final climb to Priest Pass as I stood and jammed on the pedals nearly the entire way up, sore Achilles be damned.

I fell asleep in Helena quite contentedly, but with the expectation that I would likely get knocked down a peg or three the next day as that seems to be the yin and yang of the Tour Divide.

Bike self-portrait

Cattleguards

Filtered shot of Mario and Vincent

Priest Pass at sunset

Chapter 16 – "Oh mama, I'm gonna roll,
　　　　　with a truckload of hurt.
　　　　　These wheels have rolled across
　　　　　I don't know how many bags of dirt"
　　　　　— Spin Doctors, *Bags of Dirt*

　　This chapter is dedicated to all you "gear guys" and "gear gals." You know who you are. You know every spec of every brand of every product and wait anxiously each year for *Outside Magazine* or *Ski Magazine* or *Bike Magazine* or *Playboy* to publish their annual gear buying guides. As my friends can attest, I am NOT a gear-guy. I typically do not spend much time shopping for anything, and silence or a shrug of the shoulders is my stock response when someone asks me the brand names of my tires, chain, shifters, rims, seat or derailleur as I simply do not know. When bike mechanics recommend specific parts to me, I only hear the muffled "wampwampwampwamp" sound that the teacher made in the old Charlie Brown cartoons. Additionally, I am mechanically illiterate. In fact, several years ago my mountain-biking friends affectionately and derogatorily named me "chick with car-keys" based on the generalization that most women's knowledge of cars and car-maintenance is limited to turning the key in the ignition and driving the car. I finally shed the nickname when I learned how to change tires and fix broken chains, but that is still about the extent of my repair abilities.

　　Everything changed when I committed to race the Tour Divide. I could not afford to be an idiot about my gear or maintenance abilities as there was too much at stake and a wrong decision could mean the difference between success and failure, or safety and danger. As shared earlier, I spent hours researching every single piece of Tour Divide gear, from bags to clothing to sleep system (tent, bag, pillow and pad) to hydration to bike-tools to spare bike parts to electronics to bike accessories to medical kits to steroidal butt creams (sorry, I had to end that run-on sentence somewhere and steroidal butt cream seemed appropriate). Thankfully, plenty of bikepacking gear resources and recommendations were at my fingertips, starting with my friend Bonnie Gagnon, who emailed me a spreadsheet in October 2017 containing a list of gear from her 2016 Tour Divide. I share my own gear spreadsheet as an appendix at the end of this book. However, some might find interesting the following narrative walk-through of my bike from front to back. If not, skip ahead.

　　For starters, I mentioned earlier that I equipped my bike with a Thudbuster seat-post, Brooks Saddle and Jones H-Bar for comfort. The

Jones H-Bar was also great for utility because it had nearly double the bar space because of a second metal bar which extended from each side of the front-bar to make an oval loop from which the actual handlebar grips extended. I realize my description of the H-Bar probably does not compute, so I suggest Googling "Jones H-Bar" and an image will pop right up. In short, I could attach a lot of stuff to the H-Bar, including aero-bars and padded elbow rests, two bike computers, a headlight, a Dynamo power switch, and two Revelate Design "Feedbags" which hung down on each side of my handlebar stem and which housed a can of bear spray on the right and a 24-ounce water bottle on the left. Lastly, attached to the front bar of the H-Bar was a Revelate Designs Sweetroll handlebar bag into which I stuffed my tent, inflatable sleeping pad, down vest, down jacket, toiletries, charging cords, arm-warmers, leg warmers and inflatable pillow. The Sweetroll also had a lot of different strings and cords to which I clipped my JBL Bluetooth speaker.

Attached to each leg of the front-fork (the front fork being the part that holds the front-wheel in place) were Salsa Anything Cages to which I strapped Sea to Summit dry bags containing bike tools, bike parts, spare tubes and a compact medical kit on the left, and raincoat, rain pants, waterproof socks, shower cap and ski-hat on the right.

The main reason I chose a hardtail bike with a Thudbuster seat-post over a full-suspension bike is that the suspension apparatus on a full-suspension bike fills the center frame triangle thereby greatly reducing storage options. The Timberjack has a well-sized open triangle space where I inserted a special-order three-compartment frame bag made by Rogue Panda Designs. In the main compartment on the right side of the frame bag, I carried a 4-liter bladder that was constantly filled with water during the last two weeks of the Tour because of the hot weather, dry conditions and large gaps between resupply points. In the thin second compartment on the left side of the bag, I stuffed a hand-held bike-pump, bungee cords, string, scissors and spare wheel-spokes. The bottom compartment contained a Petzl headlamp, spare batteries for my eTrex bike computer, the Anker power pack, bug-spray, and a mosquito head-net.

On the top of my top-tube (the top bar of the bike-frame that connects the seat-tube to the head-tube), I attached a Revelate Designs Mag Tank tube bag up against the head tube and a Revelate Designs Jerrycan tube bag against the seat-tube. The Mag Tank housed my power cache, my iPhone, lip-gloss, and sunscreen. The Jerrycan contained an assortment of items including Aquamira water purifying drops, a Swiss Army Knife, a bike multi-tool, extra Band-Aids, a Bic lighter and a flashing taillight.

Quick funny story about the Bic lighter. A month before the Tour, my mother bought me a two-pack of Bic lighters. For whatever reason, her bestowing upon me the ability to make fire gave her great pleasure. Three times before my departure, she checked in with me to ensure that I packed the Bic lighter. The night before I left, she called and said, "Be safe, be smart, I love you and do you have your Bic lighter?" I started wondering if the thing had magical powers based on my mother's bizarre infatuation. Mom, I am sorry to reveal that the lighter never saw the light of day or glow of moonlight. In Canada and Montana, it mostly rained and we stayed indoors. Colorado and New Mexico were in the midst of severe draughts and widespread fire-bans were in effect.

Underneath my seat (and attached to the rear of the seat-tube) was a Revelate Designs Terrapin saddlebag. Crammed into the saddlebag were my sleeping quilt, a sleeping bag liner and a dry-bag that contained my alternative clothing. This included a second pair of wool socks, a long-sleeve wool base layer, long underwear bottoms, short-sleeve wool base layer, t-shirt, and running shorts. The Terrapin also had straps on top that were great for quick exterior storage of clothes that went on and off multiple times because of changing weather such as arm-warmers, leg warmers and raincoat.

The final storage item was an Osprey Talon 11 backpack that contained a two-liter bladder. I originally anticipated using this backpack exclusively for food storage as I had plenty of other hydration options. However, that plan went out the window as soon as my two-liter plastic bottle cracked in Koko Claims' Ring of Hell on Day 2. Thereafter, the Osprey became my primary means of hydration as well as the bearer of all my daily sustenance. Speaking of sustenance, be patient. I have a whole chapter devoted to food. Just keep reading!

On the bike maintenance side, a few weeks before my departure for Canada, I spent several hours with my bikepacking/bike-mechanic guru Brian at the Bike Doctor bike shop in Frederick, Maryland. Brian gave me tutorials on replacing spokes, plugging tire holes, "truing" wheels, using chain "quick" links, replacing brake pads and screaming for help loudly and shrilly. If you live in the greater Washington D.C./Baltimore metropolitan area and are considering taking up bikepacking, go see Brian! He really knows his stuff.

The Cockpit

The Tour 'Beest'

Chapter 17 – "I've stumbled on the side of twelve misty mountains
I've walked and I've crawled on six crooked highways
I've stepped in the middle of seven sad forests
I've been out in front of a dozen dead oceans
I've been 10,000 miles in the mouth of a graveyard
And it's a hard, and it's a hard, it's a hard,
And it's a hard rain's a-gonna fall"
— Bob Dylan, *A Hard Rain's a-Gonna Fall*

Tour Divide Day 9 - 78 Miles - Helena to Butte - 7800 feet of climbing. The euphoria over our Day 8 badass century ended ingloriously with a cold wet thud. After a string of great weather since Eureka, we were due a bad day and Day 9 was royally bad. Wait, let me rephrase: Day 9 was abject torture. Our torment commenced with a restless night of sleep at the Budget Inn Express in Helena. Without exaggeration, FLEAS would lose street-cred in the insect world by staying in that dive. I slept in my sleeping bag. The thought of making skin contact with the sheets and bedspread (both of which likely pre-dated my birth in 1967) terrified me. Unfortunately, the Budget Inn Express was the only motel in the entire city of Helena with vacancy. How can that be? Well, it was a Friday night and our arrival unluckily coincided with the annual Big Sky Block Party Drag Queen Festival. Seriously. Not only was it a thing, but it was a big thing, with thousands of colorfully costumed men in drag cavorting in the streets of Helena. With apologies to my many drag queen friends, it felt like we had entered a bizarre rainbow-hued Halloween twilight zone. Okay, so I do not have any drag queen friends. That does not make me a bad person. If only I had more room in my bags for the proper attire to join the party!

Around 2AM I was awakened by a sonic boom. Thunder, followed by pouring rain. By 6AM, torrential downpour. I felt badly for those late-night drag queens who accessorized with copious quantities of make-up.

We started the day at the local Hardee's wolfing down greasy breakfast sandwiches.

A woman in line behind me at Hardee's asked, "Are you guys really riding your bikes in this weather?"

The cashier asked, "Are you guys really riding your bikes in this weather?"

An old man getting a napkin next to me asked, "Are you guys really riding your bikes in this weather?"

A woman in the booth behind us asked, "Are you fools really riding your bikes in this weather?" She overemphasized the word "fools."

Were we on *Candid Camera*?

During a break in the redundant inquisition from the Hardee's peanut gallery, we studied the route map and decided to only ride about 78 miles and end the day in the town of Butte, Montana. Even with the deluge from hell, we thought 78 miles would be a nice leisurely day after the 100+ miles the day before. We thought WRONG WRONG WRONG. For starters, it was only 47 degrees in Helena when we embarked and that turned out to be the HIGH temperature for the day. However, the more consequential issue was that three inches of overnight rain turned the dirt roads and trails to virtual quicksand and transformed small puddles into ponds. The frogs were happy. They even erected diving boards and docks along the shores of the new ponds. We, on the other hand, were not happy. We very quickly became the polar opposite of happy.

The day's ride began with a 1600-foot climb that began at the literal edge of Helena. One minute we were pedaling on a paved road passing houses, stores and gas stations in what still passed for downtown Helena. Within a mere few hundred feet, the paved road turned to dirt, the line of houses abruptly ended, and we were climbing a quiet mountain. For a relatively decent-sized city, it was unnerving how quickly urban became rural.

For a brief respite during the climb, the rain slowed to a drizzle. That changed quickly on the descent as the rain fell in sheets and the road-surface turned to a sloshy mud. Luckily, there was just enough downhill grade that we could maintain sufficient speed to prevent mud-lock (a term I coined to describe when mud is so thick that it locks your bike in place). Mud-lock is a scourge that congressional legislation should outlaw.

The next climb started immediately after completing the descent from the first climb, and ascended for 15 miles into a cloud (16 miles when considering the extra mile we rode due to a missed turn). The higher we rode, the colder it got and the less we could see. The thick clouds swallowed us. By the time we reached the peak several hours later, it was 35 bitingly cold and wet degrees. I tried to keep things light by summoning my best Bill Murray/Carl Spackler voice from *Caddyshack* and telling myself, "I don't think the heavy stuff will come down for quite a while," but humor was not warming my shivering extremities. Even our 5-star rated rainproof clothing failed miserably.

The real bummer is that the top leveled into several miles of undulating technical rocky rooty rutty wooded trail that would have been a blast to ride in dry conditions. However, the heavy rains turned long stretches of the trail into unrideable slop. Several times, I tried to power my front wheel up and over a muddy embankment only to be launched from the bike and splattered head first on the ground. By the time we reached the end of the summit slog, we were caked in mud, drenched to the bone, freezing cold, and ready to get the hell off the mountain and to the next town as quickly as possible.

Our next stop, after a ten-mile descent, was the town of Basin. As we started the descent, I looked at my compadres and apologized in advance for the waiting that I would NOT be doing. They nodded in understanding and said they would see me in Basin. I then threw caution to the hailstorm and bombed down, barely touching my brakes for the entire ten miles.

It took seven hours to cover the 40 miles from Helena to Basin. When I reached Basin's (under)world-famous Leaning Tower of Pizza, I could not feel my fingers, toes, lips, cheeks, eyelids, etc. I immediately peeled off most of my clothes and spent ten minutes practically making out with a space heater.

Noticing that I was still shivering, the waitress looked at me with abundant pity and said, "You look like you could use some hot-chocolate!"

I responded, "Make it a double and then keep them coming!"

I also ordered a couple large pizzas that escaped the oven just as the boys arrived 20 minutes later.

Once our bodies thawed, we disembarked from the Leaning Tower of Pizza and slowly waded back into the frozen cauldron. We had 38 miles to Butte, the first 20 miles consisting of a gradual climb of 1500 feet. This whole section should have been easy, but the soft conditions made riding a moderate incline feel like climbing a steep ascent. Is there a word called "trudgery?" If not, there should be as we trudged this section in drudgery.

About 10 miles into the climb, Mario and Vincent decided to take a break and told us that they would meet us in Butte. I looked at Wayne and asked, "Do you want to stop?"

Wayne shook his head and replied "Nah, I'd like to get this crap day over with as soon as possible. Let's keep on truckin'."

Wayne and I pressed on and finally reached the outskirts of Butte at 9:30PM, thoroughly torched (which is an ironic adjective for such a cold day). From an overlook perched above the town, we stared directly down an inviting paved road that descended directly into downtown Butte. But wait! Why does the red line on our Garmin show us going to the right? WTF? All we could see to the right was a dirt parking lot sitting below a steep hill. Sure enough, the red line went right through the parking lot.

Like zombies following blood, we dutifully followed the red line and found a single-track trail at the end of the parking lot that headed up the hill. We surmised that the hill probably provided an even better overlook of Butte. Because at that moment, it was supremely important that we had a better stinkin' view of Butte (there is that sarcasm again). So we climbed for ten minutes, cursed the better view, and then rode a zig-zaggy shoulder-width trail down into the heart of Butte, arriving at the Quality Inn and Suites at 10PM. Mario and Vincent arrived about 45 minutes later. 78 miles felt like 150 miles. I took no pictures until Butte, as there was nothing to see for much of the day due to the rain and fog. Regardless, my numb fingers prevented the use of gadgetry anyway.

Once checked into our rooms, we pulled a repeat of the prior evening by ordering pizza (for the third time in the last four meals) and then hosing our bikes and ourselves down with an exterior hotel hose. Worms and ants could have built entire dirt civilizations atop the hotel parking lot using the mud sprayed off our bikes and bodies. We had 311 miles left in Montana.

A cold and motley crew in Basin, MT

Overlook upon arrival in Butte

Butte

Chapter 18 – "To wreck, to wreck, to wreck,
          Did I build this ship to wreck?"
          — Florence and the Machine, *Ship to Wreck*

Tour Divide Day 10 - Butte to Wise River - 53 Miles - 5200 feet elevation gains. My eyes popped open at 5:30AM. I reached for my phone and checked the weather forecast. Bad move. Really bad move. Cold monsoonal rains had stalled over western Montana and there was no hint of sun in the forecast for another three days. Yikes. I turned over and went back to sleep. I awoke again at 7AM and checked the forecast again, hoping that the monsoon was the figment of a bad dream. No such luck. Across the room, Wayne was already gathering his things. He looked at me and said, "Get up buddy! It's time to get wet again! Isn't this great?!" I cannot remember whether I groaned, sighed or threw the hotel's digital clock at him.

After a Nordic-level invasion of the complimentary hotel breakfast bar and a stop at the local Safeway grocery store for supplies, we loaded our gear and dove tire first into the storm. Actually, we only made it ten feet from the Safeway curb when I exclaimed, "Wait! I have an idea! Give me a couple minutes." I ran back into the store and bought four pairs of rubber dishwashing gloves for each of us to wear over our bike gloves. I was a momentary hero.

Trying to keep things loose and light as we pedaled away from the Safeway, I shared with the guys the scene from the movie *Fletch* when the bad guy says to Chevy Chase (aka Fletch), "You'll be wearing rubber gloves. Do you own rubber gloves?"

Fletch replies, "I rent 'em. I have a lease with an option to buy."

Wayne emitted a brief muffled chuckle, looked at me and claimed, "You sure know a lot of movie quotes!"

"I can't help myself," I responded. "I just often think of life through movie quotes and song lyrics."

"Evidently so," replied Wayne. "Keep 'em comin'!"

Our initial goal for the day was to go 92 miles to the town of Polaris, Montana. We started south from Butte on a smooth ten miles of pavement that deposited us at the entrance of the Beaverhead-Deerlodge National Forest. The surface turned to a claylike gravel and we climbed a few thousand feet in a cold misty rain. At the top of the climb, we happened upon a public outhouse constructed of stone and noticed a bike leaning against the outhouse exterior wall. Seeking warmth, we entered the structure and found none other than Ron J, one of our fellow bunkmates from Butts Cabin back in Canada.

Huddling in the cramped space, I remarked to Ron, "We obviously share the same four-star taste in accommodations!"

Ron responded, "I love outhouse family reunions!"

We warmed our hands, shared some beef-jerky, exchanged trail stories and then ventured back out.

From the outhouse, we navigated several miles of rolling dirt roads followed by a high-velocity descent that dropped into a bovine-infested valley alongside north-south Interstate 15 before the route veered off onto another dirt road that would ascend 2300 feet to the infamous Fleecer Ridge. At the start of the march to Fleecer, Vincent and I rode ahead of the others and got to know each other better. I learned that he is finishing his education in Montreal, but most of our conversation focused on our respective years as fellow former ski-bums, 1990 in Vail for me and 2013 in Banff for Vincent.

When the climb steepened, Vincent dropped back to join Mario while I found a strong and hypnotic rhythm resulting in my separating from the group. An eerie fog encased the last few miles of the climb and obscured the peak except for a single gigantic tree near the top. There was a *Twilight-Zone* quality to the lone-tree-in-the-thick-fog-at-the-top-of-the-hill scene, especially with the final quarter mile or so of the climb passing through a treeless landscape. Approaching the tree, I half expected to find a snake dangling from a branch offering a bite from an apple! Just beyond the big tree was a nondescript right turn that led me the final few hundred yards to Fleecer Ridge, where I waited for the boys.

I mentioned earlier that the Tour Divide has several legendary and memorable locations and challenges such as Koko Claims and The Wall. The next one on the list is Fleecer Ridge, a sloppy, muddy half-mile trail that starts steeply down a 25-degree incline and then precipitously drops over a final ridge at about a 40-degree incline. Only the truly foolish attempt to ride it and, for some, their race disastrously ends there. The rest take one look from the top of the trail and intelligently walk down in the grass alongside trail. I tried to ride it. I was not aware of the steeper drop over the final ridge. The rest of the guys took one look at the trail and were instantly off their bikes. They all have higher IQs than I do.

I felt heroic on the top section. In fact, I thought, "What's the big deal and why is everyone else walking down?" Then I hit that final ridge and 'Crossed the Rubicon' as the earth (and my stomach!) abruptly dropped out from under me. At that point, the trail consisted of two parallel deep ruts. The rut on the left was u-shaped and somewhat shallow. The one on the right was v-shaped and deep. Unfortunately, I approached the final ridge in the right rut and found myself accelerating so uncontrollably that both braking and escape were impossible.

The bottom of the hill was coming fast and promised a lengthy run-out if I could just hold on for a few hundred more feet. Gulp. I made it halfway down that final drop before the rut narrowed and swallowed my front tire sending me in a swan dive over my handlebars. Greg Louganis would have been impressed. The Swedish and American judges each gave me a 9.0 on form and a 9.5 on splash, but the Russian and Syrian judges screwed me with a pair of 7s. The wipeout was an epic blur. I landed head-first in soft wet grass, my bike landed on top of me, I bounced on my hip and ass, rolled three or four times, and came to rest in a daze. Before even standing up and taking inventory of my body, my first thought was, "I hope my bike is okay." Thankfully, both my bike and my body were in one piece and I escaped with just a few keepsake bruises (including one to my ego) and a slightly rung bell. I walked the rest of the way down with my head lowered and my battered tail between my legs.

From the base of Fleecer Ridge, we rode ten miles downhill through the forest and across a few creeks. Shaken and shivering after my crash, I approached the descent gingerly. I was also concerned that I may have suffered a concussion.

We arrived in the village of Wise River just as afternoon was turning to evening. It took us over eight hours to go a measly 53 miles. A big decision confronted us. We could call it quits and shack up in a warm country inn (the Wise River Club) or we could grind out another rainy cold 39 miles to Polaris. With purple lips and chattering teeth, we chose the warmth.

Unfortunately, the warmth was limited solely to the air-temperature inside the Wise River Club as the owners of the place were anything but friendly. In fact, when we first entered the place, the proprietor (who was waiting tables in the Inn restaurant at the time) looked up at us and asked rather gruffly, "What do you want?"

We meekly responded that we would like a couple rooms.

She looked us over with a scowl and then said, "Fine, but your bikes must stay in the area below the stairs and you can't wash your clothes in the bathroom."

Nice to meet you too!

When we went back downstairs for dinner, the service did not improve as it took an hour for our food and another half hour to get our checks. At least we were warm and dry.

In hindsight, I have a little more sympathy for the Wise River Inn proprietors, but only just a little. Day 10 happened to be Father's Day and the Inn appeared to be the prime Father's Day dinner location for every family living within a 20-mile radius of Wise River. A group of wet muddy straggly unshaven men unexpectedly appearing in the restaurant seeking rooms right at the start of the dinner rush was probably unsettling, certainly distracting, and arguably unwelcome.

On the bright side, the slow dinner service gave us time to review the route map and construct a tentative plan for the next day. Since we had sacrificed hours and miles by calling it an early day, we set an ambitious plan to depart early the next morning and try to make it 138 miles to Lima, Montana, with a quick lunch-stop at the famed High Country Lodge in Polaris. From Lima, we would then make it out of Montana the following day.

We knew 138 miles would be challenging, as our longest single ride to that point was 100 miles. However, the route profile reflected some 70 total miles of pavement and only a couple long but moderate climbs over those 138 miles. We calculated that if we started at 6AM and averaged near ten miles-per-hour for the day with 'responsible' stops, we could make it to Lima by 10PM. With our delusional plan in place, we retired for the night just as the wind and rain outside reached such fury that the whole Inn shook.

Making so many new friends.

100

The Bottom of Fleecer Ridge.
This photo does not adequately depict the steepness.
I wrecked halfway down.

Chapter 19 – "Pour me something tall and strong,
  Make it a hurricane before I go insane
  It's only half past twelve but I don't care
  It's five o'clock somewhere"
  — Alan Jackson, *It's Five O'Clock Somewhere*

Tour Divide Day 11 - 40 Miles - Wise River, MT to Polaris, MT - 2800 feet of vertical. Tour de France racers are among the fittest athletes on the planet and they get a rest day each week. After ten straight grueling days, it turns out we needed one as well. The Wise River Club survived the overnight storm, but there was no let-up as cold hammering rain continued to drench western Montana into the morning. We resignedly donned our gear and headed out into the elements. To reiterate, the ambitious plan we hatched at dinner the night before was to ride 138 miles to the town of Lima with a quick stop for lunch at the High Country Lodge in Polaris at the 40-mile mark.

The first 40 miles were on a smooth tree-lined paved road that bisected the Beaver-Deerlodge National Forest. The first ten miles tilted lightly upward and Mario led the group with a fleet but comfortable pace. When the grade steepened, I ventured out well ahead. Other than a new pain in my left quad and despite the freezing cold rain, I felt great and enjoyed the quiet solitude of riding solo. My introverted pleasure heightened when I reached the top of the nearly 2,000-foot climb and the trees opened to unveil several miles of luxuriant high-mountain meadows framed beautifully on all sides by snow-capped mountains. This summit plateau then gave way to one of the most exhilarating paved descents I have ever ridden. The road contained twists and turns and steep high-speed straightaways that slingshot me into white-knuckle 180-degree switchbacks necessitating mortal combat with centrifugal force. Descending in reverie, I realized that I might have finally made peace with the foul weather.

I apparently reached Polaris at 11AM, but saw neither the High Country Lodge, nor any indication of a town. There was a post-office and a house at mile 40 and then the road returned to desolation with nary a building or telephone pole in sight. At mile 42, I turned around and scanned the road behind me. My view extended a good two miles and I saw no sign of Wayne, Mario or Vincent. I must have somehow missed the turn for the Lodge and missed the "town" of Polaris.

I rolled to a stop and contemplated my next move. I immensely enjoyed the solo serenity of the last two hours. Maybe missing the Lodge was a sign. Maybe this was the time to make a pivotal move and carry on by myself. Maybe . . . screw that! I was cold and hungry and, who's kidding who, I was no more prepared to be solo on Day 11 than I was on Day 2.

Once sanity prevailed, I backtracked past the post-office and a mile later eyed a giant sign 15 feet off the ground emblazoned with "High Country Lodge." Hanging from the sign was a model bicycle and another sign that said "Tour Divide" with an arrow pointing up the driveway to a massive wood lodge. How the hell did I miss that? In retrospect, when I rode this section 30 minutes earlier, my head was lowered to keep the rain out of my eyes and I did not start looking up until the odometer said 39.5 miles (as I thought the Lodge was at mile 40). As the Lodge was actually at mile 39, I obviously flew right past it.

By the time I ingloriously entered the Lodge, the boys had already fully unloaded their bikes and bags, disrobed and seated themselves around a table in the Lodge dining room. I was excited to be inside and warm. The interior of the Lodge was exactly how one would picture a quintessential mountain hideaway — a cavernous main area with floor-to-ceiling windows, wood paneling and wood beams everywhere, deep leather couches and chairs, stunning window views, wild animal head wall décor, and inviting aromas wafting from a nearby kitchen. While taking it all in, Mario introduced me to Russ, the amiable owner of the Lodge. Instead of a handshake, Russ handed me a giant plate of lasagna and said, "Welcome to the High Country Lodge. Dig in!"

Over lunch, we used the Wi-Fi to review the updated weather forecast, which was horrible, and learned from Russ that we would be facing intolerably muddy trail conditions over the next 98 miles and would likely end the day camping in cold wet sludge at 8,000 feet. In other words, the term "utter folly" aptly described our hopes to reach Lima that night. Russ then threw in the clincher by sharing that he had a large-load washer-dryer. Usually good food is the key to a man's heart. On the Tour Divide, clean and dry clothes are a close second.

Mario looked at me and asked, "Are you thinking what I'm thinking?"

I responded, "I am pretty sure I know what you are thinking and if you are thinking it, I can guaranty that Vincent is thinking it."

Vincent vigorously nodded yes.

"Wayne, what do you think?" I asked.

Wayne chimed in with a grin, "I think there's an awful lot of thinking going on here. I think I'm thinking what you all are thinking."

To put an end to this mid-day banquet of *Cogito, Ergo Sum* ("I think, therefore I am") and to comply with Robert's Rules of Parliamentary Procedure to make it official, I said, "All in favor of forging on, raise your hands."

No hands raised.

"All in favor of a rest day on leather couches in front of a fireplace while all of our clothes are getting washed, raise your hands."

Four hands shot up. Done. International rest day declared. In case we were feeling like wusses for this decision, Russ shared that the weather over the last three days had been the worst in the history of the race. Russ could very well have been exaggerating to generate lodging revenue, but we did not care and had no regrets.

After a lengthy hot-shower, I spent six consecutive hours melded into a soft leather couch. I took a nap, made a few phone calls, caught up on some news, took another nap, rotated an ice-pack among my various sore spots, and conducted staring contests with the various heads of dead elk, bison and moose which were mounted on the walls encircling the main room of the Lodge. Time has never raced by so quickly while doing nothing!

The afternoon rest also allowed me to take stock of our race progress. We had covered roughly 812 miles in 11 days for an average of just under 74 miles per day. That was laughably below the 90 miles per day average we needed for a 30-day finish. With over 1900 miles still to go, we would have to average over 100 miles per day from this point forward to achieve the 30-day goal. Based on the persistently bad weather and our overall progress so far, I had fleeting confidence in achieving a 30-day finish.

Covering only 93 miles in the last two days had materially set us back. We should have sucked it up and ridden the 40 miles to the Lodge the prior evening. The decision to stop at Wise River at only 6PM the day before literally cost us a full day. In the short term, stressing over a target finish date was pointless and ineffectual. With so many days and miles to go, we could not afford focusing on anything but the next day.

Late in the afternoon of our repose, two Sheilas oozed through the front door of the Lodge. No, I am not using the Australian term "Sheila" to describe a woman. They were both female racers actually named Sheila. Once they checked in and cleaned up, they joined us in the main couch area where we all shared our sundry tales of the Tour.

The Sheilas were both from Texas, one from Austin and one from San Marcos and were both Tour Divide veterans several times over. When I asked them why in the world they would want to do this race multiple times, they struggled to provide a rational explanation. They obviously suffered from what we have learned is a common Tour Divide addiction affliction. Clearly they were brave, tough and indomitable!

The Sheilas related their difficulties climbing Koko Claims and

The Wall (each making two trips up The Wall, one with their bags and one with their unladen bikes) and gave us advice and warnings about obstacles ahead. Their most chilling warning was of the infamous mud on Bannack Road, which we would face early in the next day's ride. In fact, they planned to spend the next day and night at the Lodge, while fervently hoping that the rains would move off and Bannack Road would partially dry out. I fervently hoped that the Sheilas were embellishing. I feared otherwise.

As our friendly banter continued, the subject of Tour Divide rules violations came up. I do not recall the exact context, but I think it related to my sharing the story of accepting medication from Chuck Ludden in Whitefish to relieve my screaming Achilles tendon, followed by Austin Sheila pointing out that I had broken the Tour rules by accepting "outside help." I laughed thinking she was kidding, but she gazed back at me stone-faced. I returned her gaze and remarked that I found the whole concept of rules for something like the Tour Divide to be humorously ironic. She asked quizzically, "How so?"

"Well," I responded, "the typical Tour Divide rider is someone who is crazy, rebellious, fiercely independent or otherwise dismissive of societal rules and conventions. It thus strikes me as ironic that any of us would be sticklers for dumbass rules."

Austin Sheila declared that she was not being judgmental, just sharing the facts.

I sat silently for a moment before asking Austin Sheila whether they were breaking a rule by riding together in what was supposed to be a solo race . . . a rule that Wayne, Mario, Vincent and I were also breaking.

Austin Sheila shook her head no. Apparently there is a buried rule that states that riding with another racer is "tolerated." That is probably correct when riding together is happenstance, but I'm not sure it applies to riding the race from beginning to end as part of a pre-arranged plan. Whatever, it was time for a new conversation.

Just a quick side commentary about the rules. Only the most fundamental rules concerned me, namely that I pedal all 2,731 miles of the route under my own power, take no shortcuts or deviations, and accept no motorized rides or private lodging. I was not going to win the Tour Divide, so there were no rules violations that would give me competitive advantage. Moreover, I was not competing against anyone.

I found rules against accepting trail help, meeting friends or relatives on the route, or making advance motel reservations to be arbitrary and, frankly, silly for this type of "race." To me, the Tour Divide was like the Cannonball Run, the Chinese Downhill, or the Thunder Road race in the movie *Grease*, all of which essentially operated under the mantra, "The rules are there ain't no rules!" If my attitude made me a "tourer" instead of a "racer," then so be it. If I finished the Tour Divide, the fact that I accepted electrolyte tablets from Jacki in Canada, accepted medication from Chuck in Whitefish, met Lisa in Silverthorne, or rode most of the race with Wayne, Mario and Vincent would not diminish the accomplishment one scintilla of one iota. If the race directors desired a level playing field for all competitors, then the rules should prohibit motels and commercial bike-repair services. Otherwise, racers more financially well off have an unfair advantage over those unable to afford motels or expensive bike-shop replacement parts for their bikes. I am sure there will be Tour Divide purists who scoff at this commentary, to which I say, "Mind your own business and race your own race."

Just as our rules conversation mercifully rerouted in another direction, Russ rang the dinner bell and we all happily dug into a sumptuous multi-course meal with three servings of dessert. Did I mention that Russ is the man! After dinner, we bid goodnight to Russ and our new Sheila friends and went to our rooms for an early turn-in as it sounded like we would have our hands full the next day knocking out the 98 muddy miles to Lima.

Not sure how I missed this sign

High Country Lodge

Chillin'

With Russ, High Country Lodge owner and great guy!

Chapter 20- "Waist deep in the big muddy,
Waist deep in the big muddy
You start out standing but end up crawlin'"
— Bruce Springsteen, *The Big Muddy*

Tour Divide Day 12 - 100 miles from High Mountain Lodge in Polaris to Lima, MT - 4300 vertical feet gain. On the Tour Divide, there is no such thing as just jumping out on a smooth trail and belting out an easy 100 miles. Every day has to be a (fucking) adventure. Why would Day 12 be any different? After a breakfast fit for a hockey team, Russ made us sign a big poster board containing the signatures of every 2018 Tour racer who stopped at the High Country Lodge. We then left the comfy confines of the Lodge at 7AM feeling physically and mentally rejuvenated.

The first 23 miles from the Lodge were an easy 90-minute dream. Then we turned onto the infamous Bannack Road and were jarred awake. On a normal sunny day, Bannack Road would be nothing more than a nondescript ten miles of fast dirt through cow-country. However, as Russ and the Sheilas warned us, Bannack Road was also notorious for its impassable mud when wet and it did not disappoint . . . if you are a pig. We immediately encountered thick, pasty, clog-the-drivetrain, pop-the-chain-off, curse-the-universe, cementish mud. This was even worse than the debilitating mud encountered on the descent from Koko Claims on Day 2. We labored through constant cycles (no pun intended) of churning and collecting mud, cleaning the mud off with our fingers, attempting to pedal 50 yards and then starting all over. Why not just walk the bike? Even when walking, the mud immediately stuck to and accumulated on the treads of the tires, and spread across the entire drive train. It was no different than rolling a snowball across a lawn of wet snow, expanding with each rotation until, voila, you've got yourself a snowman. With each tire rotation, the bike added seven to ten pounds of fresh mud.

Finally, after about the tenth time scraping the accumulated mud from the tires and chain, and after having yelled out every expletive in George Carlin's dictionary, I abandoned caution and reason and started pedaling in the prickly scrub brush alongside the road, despite the high risk of puncturing a tire. By then, I figured the brush would provide better traction than the soft ground. This went on for another hour before we finally hit drier surface.

It took us 90 minutes to go the first 23 miles and another 90 minutes to go a mere 1.5 miles.

Meanwhile, Wayne somehow smiled through the whole ordeal. The guy was always smiling. "Brent, good times baby!" shouted Wayne as we left the mud behind.

I tried to play along, "Yeah Wayne, it's just like being a kid and playing in the mud without a curfew. Except it's NOT!!!"

Fortunately, the REALLY muddy stuff ended around mile 27. More fortunately, there was a farmhouse at mile 27. Most fortunately, the farmhouse owners took pity by letting us use their garden hose to wash our bikes, our legs, and our shoes. In exchange for their kindness, Wayne rolled around on the ground with their dogs.

In real time, I would have preferred a nice dry Bannack Road. However, part of what makes the Tour Divide so special, epic, and memorable is dealing with and overcoming legendary obstacles like Koko Claims, The Wall, Fleecer Ridge, and Bannack Road when they are at their most monstrous. Day 12's mud on Bannack Road was just another colorful villainous character in a quixotic tale.

About a mile beyond the farmhouse, Bannack Road mercifully ended with a left onto a paved road followed a few miles later by a right turn back onto dirt. This was the beginning of a 35-mile climb up to a pass with the word "Sheep" in the name (either "Sheep Creek Divide" or maybe "Big Sheep Pass"). Everything was okay for the first few miles. It was muddy, but it was just regular slow-you-down, skid-you-around, make-you-dirty mud, not the brown Elmer's glue slop that we endured on Bannack Road. Then my chain broke at mile 37. No problem, I have fixed dozens of chains over the years. Just break the link and re-attach. Then my left quad muscle exploded (or felt like it did) at mile 42. This was the same quad muscle that started to get sore on the climb to Polaris the day before. Then I climbed eight miles in increasingly excruciating pain. With no phone service, I could not just summon an Uber.

I painstakingly pushed forward, mile after mile, until reaching a point where I could barely push my left leg through a pedal rotation. I tried to walk, but stepping hurt worse than pedaling. I sat on the ground and massaged the leg, but it was a chore to get back up. My options were limited.

As a last resort, I swapped the right flat pedal that I bought in Whitefish for my old right clipless pedal so that I could pedal almost exclusively with my right foot. This put tremendous stress on my right leg, but I had no choice but to grit my teeth and suck it up Buttercup. (As an aside, I would humorously ride the next two weeks with a flat pedal on the left side and a clipless pedal on the right.) Then at mile 55, our good friend Cole Drain (that's "cold rain" for those of you who still don't get my lame humor) showed up to accompany us for the next 3 hours. This was taking the term "embrace the suck" to a draconian level.

Strangely, I was not upset by this turn of events, just really bummed out. Over the first 11 days, I had withstood so much and survived so much that I now felt nothing but steely mental determination. However, this physical pain was so intense that I feared continuing the next day would be impossible. It is one thing to will yourself to muddle through to the end of a painful ride because you have no choice. It is something else to start a long day in that same pain.

Three miles from the summit, Wayne suggested, "Why don't you throw down some Advil."

I responded that I was still taking the pain medication that my buddy gave me in Whitefish.

Wayne sarcastically remarked, "Yeah, that's working out really well for you."

"Right," I muttered. Figuring I had nothing to lose (besides stomach lining), I relented and gobbled five 200 milligram Advil caplets.

Apparently, the scenery was great at the top of Big Sheep whatever, but I was too far deep in the pain-cave to notice and/or care. Even the descent was tormenting as we only dropped 1,000 feet over 30 miles and, because of the soft ground, there was not enough declining gradient to coast without agonizing pedaling.

Thankfully, the mega dose of Advil kicked in halfway down and the pain abated over the last 15 miles into Lima, where we found accommodations at the Mountain View Motel & RV Park. This motel was pure gold from a Tour Divide standpoint as it provided us with a garden hose AND a washer/dryer. Clean clothes and clean bikes made for clean minds . . . or something like that. Okay, I just made that up.

Later that evening, as I sat with an ice pack on my leg while indulging in a calorie-fest at Jan's Café across the street from the motel, I thought about how great this adventure would be if it simply got just a teensy weensy little bit fun again. Seriously, was that too much to ask? The four days in a row of cold rain and mud had worn me down and the quad issue on the Pass of the Giant Lamb had shaken me. I do not pray, but I strongly hoped that my quad would magically improve overnight as the prospect of spending an extra day or two in Lima while my boys rode off into the sunrise was depressing. Besides, the next day would be momentous. After holding us hostage for the past four days, Montana would finally release us!

I could not wait to get to Idaho and then Wyoming. I could not wait for better weather. I could not wait for dry ground. As I reclined on my creaky mattress, I reminded myself that every 100 miles ridden resulted in a new $1400 in mileage pledge donations to First Descents. I had to keep fighting because I could keep fighting. Far too many people in the world do not have that ability, choice, or option. With First Descents on my mind, I remembered that I still had a few unread letters from my January plea. So I grabbed my phone, opened my "First Descents Letters" file, and read the following letter from my dear friend April "Lemon Drop" Capil:

> *Dear Sunday,*
>
> *You would think the moment my life changed forever would have been the moment I found out I had cancer. It was not, though. That feeling of your world tipping on its axis actually happened several months later, when I was sitting down with my new oncologist. She was a smart woman, a serious woman, and I knew my life – for all intents and purposes – was in good hands. "With triple negative cases like yours," she was telling me, "I like to recommend a clinical trial, because there isn't anything you can take to keep it from coming back." The air went out of the room then, because I was not sure I had heard her right. Coming back? I thought. What did she mean, coming back?*
>
> *That moment was the first time someone told me the truth: that contrary to all the pink ribbons and walks for a "cure," triple-negative breast cancer was not something I could "beat." We do not have a cure; we do not have a vaccine or a targeted therapy that eliminates the possibility of its return. Its return, in fact, is usually within 2 to 3 years of diagnosis, and when it comes back, it's usually fatal. That moment in her office was the first time I realized the most I could hope for was "NED": No Evidence of Disease. Remission would not be the crushing victory I had imagined – it would be a state of withdrawal, a state where the handful of renegade cells that had started a small rebellion in my body were no longer actively trying to kill me. We would do our best, she said, to shut their coup d'état down with petrochemicals and radiation, but, like the scrappy heroes of Star Wars, they could survive, siloed somewhere beyond an MRI's reach, waiting for the right conditions to thrive again.*

No one told me, when I was diagnosed, that I would never again live without cancer – without an awareness of the possibility of recurrence. That I would never enjoy the peace of mind that 20-somethings and non-hypochondriacs wake up with every day. I had my last chemo treatment almost a decade ago, but every muscle twinge, every upset stomach or headache reminds me of my mortality, my fallibility. It has been a mixed blessing, this awareness of my body's imperfection, my life's unpredictability. At first, it manifested as the bucket list to end all bucket lists – a five-year period where I did everything I was afraid I would not get to do before I died. I ran the New York Marathon, moved to a new city, wrote two books and climbed Kilimanjaro. If cancer was going to take me, I told myself, it was not going to be without a fight. But after five years – after the odds of a recurrence were the same as the odds of a non-survivor, I was left with what most people have: the rest of my life. I asked a nurse, "But... what if it comes back?" She looked at me with kind eyes and said, "What if it doesn't?"

It was First Descents that gave me that double-edged H-Bomb of survivorship: Hope. The thing with feathers, that perches in the soul, that sings the tune without the words and never stops at all. First Descents did not teach me to fight cancer. It taught me to fight resignation. Apathy. Entropy. Those villains of life that keep you from out living it. First Descents taught me how to climb and kayak, but more importantly, it taught me how to live. How to live like someone who gets to live. First Descents taught me how to fight the feeling that I can't do this, that it's too hard or I'm too tired or I don't have it in me. What I know because of First Descents is that I do have it in me. That I can dig deep, and persevere, and when I do, my strength will meet me in that place where my hope is threatened, and I will triumph. I may not be able to stop a recurrence, or a corporate takeover, or the crow's feet that come with 40 years of laughing, but because of First Descents, I know I can outlive these things – I can bear the slings and arrows of outrageous fortune and still be *thankful for the time I have, however borrowed it may be.*

My dear, brave Sunday: when you are facing an uphill climb on your journey, remember this: we are part of a family that knows when you listen, you will hear that voice of strength and hope within you, and it will carry you up whatever mountain you need to summit. I believe in you, treasure you, and send you out into the world with all the hope and strength First Descents reminded me I have in me. THANK YOU for everything you do for First Descents and for so many young survivors whose lives you have changed and will continue to change.

Dig Deep. You can do this. It is not too hard. You are not too tired. You do have it in you.
All my love, Lemon Drop

With a full heart, I closed my eyes, smiled, and drifted off to sleep. I may hurt, I may bitch and moan, I may feel lower than low and go slower than slow, but absent calamity, there was no way in hell I was not going to finish this infernal race.

Wayne playing with dog. Best moment of the day.

Chapter 21 – "Cheeseburger in paradise,
　　　　 Heaven on earth with an onion slice
　　　　 Not too particular, not too precise,
　　　　 I'm just a cheeseburger in paradise"
　　　　 — Jimmy Buffet, *Cheeseburger in Paradise*

A question repeatedly asked throughout the race via social media was, "What do you eat all day and where do you get your food?" The easy answer to the first part of the question is calories, calories and more calories. For example, my Day 12 menu included a breakfast of four scrambled eggs, six pancakes, four pieces of bacon, hash browns and a bagel, followed by two protein bars and a blueberry muffin during the morning ride, a turkey sandwich, Snickers bar and apple pie for lunch, three more protein bars and four pop-tarts in the afternoon, a peanut butter and jelly sandwich and two chocolate-chip cookies in the late afternoon, another protein bar and half a bag of beef jerky an hour after the PBJ, and a cheeseburger, fries, extra fries, extra cheeseburger and ice cream for dinner. The Tour Divide is more of a Food Divide punctuated by some biking! It was impossible to ingest as many calories as we burned each day. I lost five to seven pounds over the first two weeks and would go on to lose another five to seven pounds by the end.

　　Most of our meals came courtesy of local convenience stores, but we occasionally enjoyed hot sit-down meals when arriving in towns at the right time of day. Proper planning was essential to ensure sufficient hydration and nutrition. I constantly calculated the distances and times to the next resupply points and then further calculated my calorie and fluid intake needs between those points. In my prior one-day race experience, my body cooperated best during long efforts when I consumed an average of between 250 to 300 calories and 24-30 ounces of fluids per hour. To be safe on the Tour, I loaded my pack based on the formula of 300 calories and 24 ounces of fluids multiplied by the maximum number of hours until the next resupply point. If the next store or restaurant was a maximum of 8 hours away, then my goal was to find 2400 calories worth of food and 180 ounces of fluids.

　　When entering a store, the first visit was invariably to the freezer to inspect the selection of frozen burritos. Burritos were not only a great source of calories, carbs and proteins, but they lasted for days and were easy to stuff in a backpack. Two pop-tarts provided 380 calories. That was a perfect snack to provide an hour of energy. Chuck Lee (introduced on Day 13) and I were connoisseurs of honey buns and processed dry desserts.

We joked about how typical moderately healthy consumers inspect food wrappers to select foods with the least calories. Chuck and I searched for foods with the MOST calories. To illustrate, I might hit the dessert shelf and find a boxed apple-pie loaded with 350 calories. An instant later, Chuck might yell my name from across the store: "Brent! Jackpot! I found a honey bun with 475 calories!!"

For hydration, I predominantly relied on water mixed with electrolyte tablets during the first half of the race (except for my epic failure to use electrolytes during days 1 and 2). In Canada, Montana and northern Wyoming, I did not need to tote much water, as there were plenty of streams to fill a bladder and purify the water. However, as the race wore on and the terrain and climate dried, we had to rely on store-bought products or water from the motel sink. In addition, as cumulative exhaustion set in, I increased my reliance on excessive amounts of Gatorade, Coke and Dr. Pepper to sustain me. I ran out of electrolyte pills early in New Mexico and could not find replacements anywhere. I resorted to buying six bottles of Gatorade per stop and filling my two bladders with the stuff. I joked that I was a sugar diabetic and caffeine addict by the end of the race and would need to formally detox, as I do not indulge in soft drinks in real life and have not experienced a steady flow of caffeine since my law-firm days in my late 20s. One thing that shocked my riding cohorts is that I have never had a cup of coffee in my life!

The last food items to become mainstays late in the Tour, thanks to Wayne, were popsicles and Swedish Fish. I consumed an average of six popsicles and a bag of Swedish fish per day by the last week of the Tour. With the popsicles, it did not matter whether it was morning, afternoon or evening, and I had no flavor preferences. Wayne was the king of popsicles. He ate three or four at one sitting . . . and always with a smile.

Surprisingly, we ate minimal traditional "fast-food." We ate breakfast in a McDonalds in Fernie on the morning of Day 3 and breakfast at Hardees in Helena on the morning of Day 9. After that, we did not see another fast-food joint until we feasted in a McDonalds in Cuba, New Mexico on Day 26. That meal in Cuba set a new craving in motion that resulted in McDonalds stops in Grants, New Mexico on Day 27 and Silver City, New Mexico on Day 29. As with caffeine and soda, I never eat fast food in real life. The Tour Divide was the ultimate free pass!

Just a sampling of an average day in my backpack!

Chapter 22 - "Hoo Hoo Hoo Hoo Hoo Hoo Hoo Hoo Hoo
You're living in your own Private Idaho
Living in your own Private Idaho
Underground like a wild potato"
— B-52s, *My Own Private Idaho*

Tour Divide Day 13 - 103 miles - Lima, MT to a marsh in Idaho. After what seemed like a month detained as an inmate of Montana, we finally made our escape on Day 13 and immediately requested political asylum in Idaho. The assholes at Montana central command did everything they could do to forestall our liberation, including bogging us down in several more miles of muddy roads and pummeling us with a rainsquall two miles before the Idaho state line. Happily, our run for the border (also our seventh crossing of the Continental Divide) succeeded at 5:45PM mountain standard time on Wednesday, June 20th. We were free!

The day started with a delectable pancake breakfast back at Jan's Cafe where I spent a solid 30 minutes icing and massaging my quad. That must have done the trick. Although it was sore at the start, I felt none of the intense and acute pain from the day before. More promising was that the quad loosened up in the first hour of pedaling. In retrospect, I think I severely overworked the muscle when grinding through the mud on Bannack Road and it essentially said "NO MAS" and shut down. Of course, that is a law degree diagnosis, not medical degree.

Our departure from Lima was also notable as Chuck Lee joined us after breakfast. Chuck was a co-participant of Wayne's from the 2016 TransAmerica race. He had been chasing us for days and was thrilled to share the experience with fellow riders. Chuck, by the way, is 68 years old and the friendliest guy in the world. I was initially a little concerned about the changing dynamics of a new rider, but I ultimately grew quite fond of Chuck as he rode off and on with us through Pie Town, New Mexico on Day 28.

The last stretch of Montana from Lima to the Idaho border consisted of 71 miles of flat (by Tour standards) dirt roads that ran eastward through a valley between two mountain ranges. We trudged through several stretches of sloppy mud, but nothing as sinister as Bannack Road, and we enjoyed a relatively dry day except for a brief squall a few miles before the Idaho border. We also hit the 1,000-mile mark a few miles before the border. In the words of my sister, "Amazeballs!"

Montana's last hurrah was a steep 300-foot climb over Red Rock Pass where, upon arrival, we high-fived, whooped and hollered, and generally partied like it was June 2018.

Once in Idaho, the sun came out, the angels sang, the cicadas rejoiced, and we hit a flowy four to five mile trail in the woods that deposited us in the town of Sawtelle at mile 86. After a five-star dining experience at L'Auberge de Subway and some grocery shopping, we headed out for two more hours on an old sandy rail trail known as the "Rail Trail" and stopped to camp at mile 103.

Reaching Idaho was an important milestone on the Tour Divide. Apparently, Tour Divide statistics reveal that if a racer makes it out of Montana, his/her odds of completing the race shoot up from 40% to 80%. Considering everything that I had endured over the first 13 days, including almost every biblical plague, I finally believed that I could lend support to those odds and finish this thing.

15 miles west of Lima

Lunch time

Lunch time

Group cheer upon leaving Montana

Goodbye Montana; Hello Idaho

Bridge on the Rail Trail

Idaho marsh

Chapter 23 – "Sometimes, when the spirit moves me, I can do many wondrous things"
— Van Morrison, *Did Ye Get Healed?*

Tour Divide Day 14 - 95 miles - Targhee Forest, ID to Heart Six Ranch, WY. To successfully get through the Tour Divide, one must have a modicum of amnesia to forget about the pain-and-misery days, and sufficient discipline to not look past tomorrow as the scale of the race is simply too overwhelming. All one can do is live in the now and Day 14's "now" was spectacular.

The day started shakily as our campsite was in a low-lying area and everything we owned was drenched when we awoke. While donning my wet shorts, wet jersey and wet gloves, I silently questioned the appeal of this camping thing! Fortunately, the beauty of the day unfolded quickly with cloudless skies and rapidly warming temperatures.

The riding commenced with a 25-minute warm-up over the last five miles of the Rail Trail (which we renamed "Mosquito Alley" . . . because there were a shit-ton of mosquitos and because we are so clever). At the end of the Rail Trail, we stopped at an opening in the forest that offered our first glimpse of Wyoming's imposing and magnificent Grand Tetons 50 miles to the southeast.

Shortly thereafter, a humorous episode ensued as we reached a spot where about 40 yards of foot-deep water submerged the entire trail. With marsh on each side of the trail, there were no bypass options. Wayne and I nonchalantly shrugged, plowed into the water, pedaled until our feet were fully submerged, hopped off our bikes, and waded through to the other side. Mario and Vincent were afraid of melting if they got wet, so they produced and starred in an off-Broadway production consisting of removing their shoes and socks, stowing them in their packs, wading through to the other side in their bare feet, drying off their feet, and putting everything back on, all while tolerating merciless heckling from Wayne and me. Fifteen minutes after reaching the water crossing, they were finally ready to go . . . until Vincent discovered that he had dropped his gloves. Pointing to the other side of the water and uproariously laughing, Wayne said, "Uh Vince, would those be your gloves on the trail back there?"

Vincent followed Wayne's finger and gaze and could only respond, "SHIT!"

"Damn, looks like your gloves are mocking you Vince," continued Wayne, unwilling to let it rest.

Mario, being the good dad, took everything off again, waded back through the water, grabbed the gloves, returned through the water, dried his feet again, and put his shoes and socks back on again. By then, Wayne and I had completed the New York Times crossword puzzle (weekend edition) and our feet were dry!

Unadulterated joy best describes the next 15 miles as we descended through an aromatic pine forest on a double-track trail sitting high on the cliffs overlooking Idaho's Warm River. I had never heard of the Warm River, but its pristine beauty stunned me.

We next connected to the Targhee National Forest and climbed up and into Wyoming. Sadly, there was no welcome sign. We did not even realize we were in Wyoming until I received a congratulatory text from my dot-watching friend Gary Morris. I texted Gary back and asked how long we had been in Wyoming. He responded, "At least an hour."

From Targhee, we made our way to the Flagg Ranch visitor center and campground where we came face to face for the first time with a curious species known as 'vacationing tourists.' Though we knew assimilation with these folks would be nearly impossible (not to mention mentally hazardous), we did our best to behave and not offend.

On the porch of the visitor center, we met a couple from Texas who was touring the northwest in an RV. The conversation was very predictable as it was identical to dozens of conversations that we had with "civilians" through the Tour:

Tourists: "Those are some cool bikes ya got there. Where are y'all comin' from?"
Us: "Banff, Alberta, Canada."
Tourists: "Wow, that's a long way. And where are y'all going?"
Us: "The US/Mexico border at Antelope Wells, New Mexico."
Tourists: "Whaaaaat?? Are you all insane? Why are you doing that?"
Us, scratching our heads: "That's a damn good question."
All: Chuckle chuckle

As usual, we spent far too long at the Flagg Ranch as they had a small lobby alcove furnished with comfy leather chairs that far outcomfied our faux-leather bike seats.

From Flagg Ranch, we swung around north of the Tetons and then south alongside the Tetons with gripping views over Jackson Lake. Along the pristine shoreline of the lake, we stopped and took a signature photo of the five of us.

As dusk settled in, we passed the village of Moran, Wyoming. Minutes later, we rounded a curve and saw an array of Indian tipis planted on a hillside plateau in the distance. As we neared the assemblage of tipis, we discovered that they were part of a small resort called the Heart Six Ranch. We had no lodging plans for the night and were unsure about our camping prospects farther up the road, so we stopped at the ranch office and inquired about the Tipis. Lucky us! They had two available Tipis for the night, with each one containing three beds. SOLD! Mario and Vincent grabbed the first one and Wayne, Chuck and I grabbed the second one.

Finding the tipi resort turned out to be propitious, as we would have otherwise camped in dank tents. I had completely forgotten about the dew from that morning until we unpacked our bikes and Chuck, doing his best Indian tribal elder imitation, said, "I suggest that we use this opportunity to dry out the tents." I removed mine from the bag and it was still dripping wet. Chuck was a sage man and was already earning his keep (until he started snoring in the middle of the night)!

Before going to sleep, I reflected on the whirlwind last three days since leaving the High Country Lodge. Over that stretch, we covered 300 miles and the cumulative fatigue of the Tour was now palpable. In addition to general exhaustion, I was bruised, scratched, bit-up, sunburned, chapped, numb in a few fingers, and sore in multiple places (including a place we do not like to talk about). However, I felt extreme gratification that I was taking this journey and again recognized that any hardships I suffered paled in comparison to the cancer hardships suffered by those for whom this ride benefited. The final thought I had before drifting off to sleep was, "Holy shit, tomorrow starts week 3 and we aren't even halfway to the finish!"

Soaking wet campsite

Our first view of the Tetons

Mario and Vincent crossing the pond

Warm River overlook

Targhee National Forest

Heart Six Ranch, Moran, Wyoming

Jackson Lake and the Tetons
(Chuck, Brent, Wayne, Mario, Vincent).

Chapter 24 – "Everybody's got a mountain to climb
Don't be discouraged when the sun don't shine
Gotta keep on pulling; you gotta keep on tryin'"
— Allman Brothers, *Everybody's Got a Mountain to Climb*

Tour Divide Day 15 - 83 miles- Moran, WY to somewhere in the wilderness. Alec Baldwin once tweeted, "Some days you're the kid with the stick, some days you're the piñata." I started Day 15 as the kid with the stick and ended the day as the piñata! We left our homey tipis at 7AM and inhaled a quick breakfast at the ranch's attached restaurant called the Buffalo Valley Café. After breakfast, we loosened up with a gentle ten-mile warm-up ride to a rustic lodge called Turpin Meadow, followed by a relaxed and serene 1700-foot wilderness climb up to another bucolic resort called the Togwotee Mountain Lodge. Known to the public as a premier snowmobiling destination in the winter, the Togwotee Mountain Lodge is known to me for the diverse offering of frozen burritos offered at its small convenience store.

From Togwotee we climbed another 1,000 feet along a paved highway to an unnamed pass on the Continental Divide where we met some motorcyclists who were riding from Houston, Texas to Alaska. They complimented our bikes while one remarked, "Thank Gawd our bikes have 1,800 cc engines!"

Just beyond the unnamed pass, we took a left onto a slightly hidden dirt road and blasted through a stimulating five-mile section of dirt, rocks and snow, before earning one of the best descents on the entire Tour Divide. Not only was it ten miles of mirthful downhill, but the road surface was a tacky-smooth lightly traveled winding dirt road with scenery fit to jump off a postcard or the pages of *Outside Magazine*. Early in the descent, we passed a horse farm situated between the road and a mountain adorned by a thick forest of pine trees overshadowed by a wall of towering snow covered rock escarpments. I hate braking during a full-speed descent, but I stopped to marvel at this view (and take a picture of course).

At the bottom of the descent, we rolled into yet another inviting country resort called Lava Mountain Lodge. At Lava Mountain, we hungrily devoured sandwiches, cookies, pop-tarts and candy. Additionally, we restocked our food supplies, as it was 92 miles before the next supply point in Pinedale, WY.

Just as we were about to set sail from the resort, a rapidly moving storm cloud passed over, delaying our departure for ten minutes. This was not otherwise notable but for the fact that this was the last sustained rain we would encounter on the Tour Divide . . . which was pretty nuts considering we still had over two weeks and 1500+ miles of riding to go AND considering the monsoons we so recently endured.

   The next two hours consisted of a series of steeper and steeper climbs, including one hike-a-bike section on a narrow rooty rocky trail that rose 600 vertical feet in under a half-mile and made The Wall in Canada seem like a bunny slope. In other words, it was HEINOUS! Twice I took a wrong step in the steep loose rocks and slid several feet downhill. Once I nearly toppled over backwards. During the hike, I also noted that my upper-body strength had weakened in the two weeks since Koko Claims and The Wall. This made for an exhausting and curse-laden push, especially since none of the maps or literature (or the Sheilas) alerted us to this torment. Apparently, this stretch was a recent Tour Divide-specific reroute from the official ACA (Adventure Cycling Association) Great Divide mapped route.[4] I should have known. The guys who sent us up this climb were the same fuckers who thought Koko Claims would be a good idea in lieu of the easier ACA-prescribed route to Fernie.

   Thankfully, our toil earned reward. The trail exited the forest into a vast clearing that led up to a ridge known as Union Pass. Our jaws dropped and our senses overloaded atop Union Pass. The ridge ran for several miles above tree line and provided us with 360-degree views of the Tetons to our northwest, the Cathedral Mountains to our northeast, the Wind River Range to our southeast, the Bridger-Teton National Forest to our southwest, and a massive rainbow to our east. At 9,750 feet in elevation, Union Pass was the highest point of the Tour Divide thus far.

   As a quick side story, Mario displayed his true strength on one of the steep climbs before the hike-a-bike. Typically, Mario and Vincent lagged behind Wayne and me on climbs. Although Mario exhibited his power leading a few pace lines in Montana, he had yet to leave Vincent behind and attack a climb. Until today. In short, he effortlessly cleaned a steep two-mile section that forced Wayne and me off our bikes. By the time Wayne and I reached the top, Mario was waking up from a nap. Okay, slight exaggeration, but Mario was a badass!

   From Union Pass, we descended several miles on a treacherous, rocky, and rutted double-track trail followed by 15 miles of rolling hills on a gravel road that meandered across a mountaintop meadow. This section

---

4   *The ACA mapped a standard route down the Continental Divide known as the "Great Divide Mountain Bike Route" or "GDMBR." Roughly 95% of the Tour Divide race follows the GDMBR. The other 5% consists of diversions and alternate routes that change from year to year due to weather conditions or route issues (such as road closures, forest closures or downed bridges).*

was visually stimulating, but endless. According to my Garmin, we were still at 9,500 feet of elevation. Evening had arrived and light was fading. At some point, a 1,500 foot descent would drop us into a valley where we would stop and set up camp. However, since we were on an alternate Tour Divide-specific route rather than the Great Divide route illustrated in the ACA maps, we did not know when we would reach the descent.

Each time we labored, grunted and grinded our way up a hill, we crested with optimism that our day's climbing was *finito*. But then, after a brief descent, the trail inevitably flattened and rose again. This monotonous cycle of uphill effort followed by a quick downhill respite followed by another uphill effort ripped my legs apart. Despite having climbed over 7,500 feet for the day, at that moment I would have preferred a single several thousand foot sustained climb to the continuous rollers numbering well into the teens.

By the time we mercifully reached the final big descent, I could barely turn the pedals over. My legs were crushed. I had become the piñata. While a 1500-foot descent usually excites the hell out of me, this one was just more hard work. The trail was in treacherous shape with deep rocky parallel ruts. Staying upright while traveling at high speeds in and out of the ruts required intense concentration. The dimming light only added to the precariousness. The death-grip on my hand brakes only added to the numbness in my fingers. This was a rare descent without smiles.

We finally leveled out in the valley below Union Pass (still at 8,000 feet elevation) and rolled to a stop along a flat grassy area next to the trail. The clock said 9:10PM, darkness was encompassing the valley, and it was time to stick a three-pronged fork in the day. We only covered 83 miles due to the sheer volume of elevation gain coupled with the exhausting hike-a-bike sections. It was an incredible day, but the piñata was beaten and torn asunder.

I do not remember falling asleep that night. It was that quick.

One additional side note: We were blissfully ignorant about grizzly danger in the valley where we camped. In stories and blogs that I read following the Tour Divide, veteran riders commonly advise that riders should NEVER EVER camp in the 40-ish mile stretch between Union Pass and the paved road that leads to Pinedale, Wyoming. Apparently, this stretch is famous for "angry troublemaking bears" that are relocated to this unpopulated area by the National Park Service from the touristy Yellowstone National Park. Rookies . . .

Horse farm that struck my fancy

Lava Mt Lodge - lunch break

Rear-view

Mario under the rainbow

Descending from Union Pass

Mosquito netting - Best purchase for Tour Divide

Chapter 25 – "The wind knows the songs of the cities and canyons
The thunder of mountains, the roar of the sea
The wind is the taker and giver of mornings
The wind is the symbol of all that is free"
— John Denver, *Windsong*

Tour Divide Day 16 - 130 Miles - Wyoming wilderness to Atlantic City, WY. The mental highs and lows of the Tour Divide are only exceeded by the actual highs and lows of the terrain. I greeted Day 16 in a funk. For starters, we slept at 8,000 feet and froze our asses off. Despite wearing every layer of clothing I carried with me, I shivered uncontrollably in my quilt from 3AM to 6AM. Additionally, I was breaking down from all of my maladies, each one painful enough to sideline me for one to two weeks under normal circumstances. A new infirmity blossomed shortly after lunch the prior day when my right knee started aching and worsened as the day progressed. Crawling out of my tent on Day 16, the knee hurt to the touch. I concluded that the injury resulted from the constant re-positioning of my feet and saddle, first performed to protect and manage my left Achilles tendon issue (which popped up on Day 4), and then my left quad issue (which popped up on Day 12).

My body (and my brain) had thus far shown a respectable resilience to pain, so I hoped to deal with this new knee irritation as I had dealt with the other afflictions. However, between the pains, the major miles covered over the prior four days, and the teeth-chattering night of half-sleep, I felt mentally and physically fried. I did my best to mask my grumpiness as we packed our bikes for departure.

We left the campsite at 8:30AM and plodded 40 boring miles to Pinedale. I say "plodded" because we felt no urgency. I do not know whether to blame the cold morning or general malaise, but for the first time on the Tour, we failed to formulate a mileage or end-destination plan before setting off.

The highlight of this section was encountering two road cattle-crossings . . . the first of which starred a group of 'city folk' on a *City Slickers* vacation. Regrettably, we did not see the ghost of Curly. Approaching the outskirts of Pinedale, a second cattle crossing stopped us in our tire-tracks. While awaiting the last dawdling heifers to reach the other side of the road, my mind wandered to another movie scene referencing cows, this time *Blazing Saddles*. In the scene, Hedley Lamarr (played by Harvey Korman) interviews outlaws to invade the town of Rock Ridge and asks one of the outlaws to recite his criminal qualifications.

The outlaw responds, "Stampeding cattle."

Hedley smirks and says, "That's not much of a crime."
To which the outlaw further responds, "Through the Vatican."
Hedley says, "Kinky! Sign here."
Pinedale bore no resemblance to the Vatican, but when in Rome . . .

Speaking of cows and cattle, I should have started a cow-counting game back at the U.S. border in Montana. The sheer number of cow inhabiting the American west is staggering. They are omnipresent. I met brown cows, black cows, white cows, red cows, multi-colored cows, spotted cows, cows with horns, cows with crazy big udders, cows with large droopy ears, cows with tiny ears, mama cows with their calves, fat cows, skinny cows, loud cows, sleeping cows, curious cows, ambivalent cows, multi-lingual cows, branded cows, wild cows, leader-of-the-pack cows, sniveling cows, sighing cows, vacationing cows and depressed cows seemingly resigned to their fates. I saw exponentially more cows than humans and easily more cows than the total number of miles ridden on the Tour. Playing the game would have been a productive and fun diversion.

Usually fencing or cattle guards in the roads confined or restricted my bovine friends. However, plenty of these gentle creatures freely roamed alongside us, in front of us and/or behind us. And they all shopped at the same earring store . . . the one that sells plastic earrings with engraved numbers. Who started that business? And despite their fat and slow appearance, cows are surprisingly nimble. Not one single cow failed to leap quickly aside upon our approach. Some even ran next to us for hundreds of yards, matching or exceeding our speeds. I assumed it was fast-twitch interval training prescribed by their race coaches.

We spent two and a half hours in Pinedale gorging on a gourmet pasta lunch, picking up supplies (including a box that I sent to the Pinedale post office before the Tour that contained replacement gloves and more steroidal butt cream), and generally lollygagging. Okay, it was not really gourmet, but other than Russ's High Country lasagna, we had not seen pasta since Fernie, so it looked and tasted gourmet. We reviewed the ACA maps at lunch and assumed that we would ride another 40-50 miles and then camp out in the Wind River Valley. Meanwhile, my right knee was now aflame. While icing it, I announced that I might only ride another 11 miles to the town of Boulder, WY and check into a motel. Dr. Wayne advised me, "Gobble a 'bunch' of Advil and you'll be fine!" There is nothing like a yummy ibuprofen dessert.

Then the stars aligned and Tour Divide karma finally swung our way. Leaving Pinedale, a forceful and direct tailwind propelled us with alacrity. Barely blinking, we covered 40 miles in under three hours, the first 20 miles on pavement and the next 20 on a lonely windswept road thrusting us smack into the heart of the Wind River Valley.

Words fail to describe adequately the desolate beauty of Wyoming's Wind River Valley. I spoke to friends before the Tour who described the Wind River Valley as their favorite place on earth to discover peace, solitude, nature, adventure and vastness. To my delight, I found truth in that assessment. Resplendent natural eye candy was visible in every direction, around every curve of the road, and over every small rise in the terrain. We headed in a southeasterly direction on a jeep road flanked by the jagged snowcapped Wind River Range to the north, and cattle ranches, sagebrush pastures, small tree-lined creeks, and open expanse to our south. The vibrant rays of the setting afternoon sun created such a magical visual tapestry that we all rode extended stretches in awestruck silence. Adding to the reverie were ominous dark clouds that framed the mountains above us, but which were sufficiently distant to pose no threat.

For me, deafening silence defined the Wind River Valley. There were no cars, engines, airplanes, people or other sounds associated with civilization. Eerily, there were also no animal or bird sounds. The only sound was the song of the wind. I even killed my own music to engage more fully in the hypnotic silence. I tried imagining the feeling of riding through that valley solo. I would have felt like the only person on earth.

Still enjoying a brisk tailwind, we covered another fast 25 miles and, by 7:30PM, had ridden 105 miles for the day. We stopped atop a plateau for a quick snack, my 48th burrito of the Tour Divide, and opened the ACA map to review our options for the night. To our surprise, we were only 25 miles from the town of Atlantic City, WY, the gateway to the Great Basin of Wyoming. With no cell service, I texted Lisa on the satellite device and asked her to jump on her computer and find us two rooms in the town. Utilizing Lisa as a travel-concierge technically constituted my third rules violation of the Tour (see my rules commentary in Chapter 19). Yawn. Within minutes, Lisa responded that we were booked at a bed and breakfast called "Wild Bill's." Lisa rocks the Casbah!

At our rate of travel, we visualized a cozy dinner at Wild Bill's by 9PM. Tour Divide proverb #23: cockiness often leads to a swift kick in the teeth. Soon after starting those final 25 miles, the route veered north dead into a howling wind. Additionally, we reeled from the sucker-punch of a series of relentlessly steep rolling climbs and descents that did not appear on the map. Instead of relaxing in front of a fireplace by 9PM, the last 25 miles took two and a half hours with the last hour unnervingly journeyed in complete darkness punctuated only by flashes of distant lightning and the incandescent glows of our four headlamps.

    We descended into Atlantic City to find neither the Atlantic, nor a city. It was barely even a village. However, we located Wild Bill's at 10:30PM and wearily pulled our bikes up to the front entrance. Like an apparition, a silver-haired, bearded gentleman suddenly materialized and welcomed us with a hearty, "Good evening gents! We have been waiting up for you! I am Wild Bill and I welcome you to my humble abode. It is late, so please keep it quiet as others are sleeping."

    Wild Bill related that when Lisa called, he initially told her that he had no rooms available as he was holding them for Tour Divide riders. When she shared that she needed the rooms for Tour Divide riders (i.e., us), he turned into the Gatekeeper in the *Wizard of Oz* who, when Dorothy asks to see the Wizard and shows him her red slippers, says, "Well bust my buttons! Why didn't you say that in the first place? That's a horse of a different color! Come on in!"

    I know, I know, that is three movie references in one day. It was that kind of day. Regardless, it was a day that ended with us lodging with the real-life Gatekeeper at the entrance to the Great Basin.

    Bill showed us to our cabins and told us to get some sleep and then get our butts to the dining room for a 6:30AM breakfast. Everything sounded great. We were tired and cold (it was 38 degrees), but thrilled to shower, sleep in beds, and meet one of the true characters (and legends) along the Tour Divide route. Moreover, we were very satisfied by the 130-mile effort (the longest ride of my life) after only managing 83 miles the day before. I was particularly gratified considering that I entertained quitting for the day after just 50 miles. The human body is a marvel.

    A couple other endnotes to the day. An hour after our arrival, a howling thunderstorm rolled through the area. That would have been horrifying in a tent. Additionally, Wild Bill's B & B doubles as a gun shop with enough artillery to arm a small militia . . . which is ironic considering Atlantic "City" is essentially a quiet street with no more than 50 residents within a three square mile radius.

Tour Divide meets City Slickers

Wind River Valley

Wind River Valley

Wind River Valley

Wild Bill's B and B, Atlantic City, WY

The Man, myth and legend - WILD BILL

Chapter 26– "I've been through the desert on a horse with no name
It felt good to be out of the rain
In the desert you can remember your name
'Cause there ain't no one for to give you no pain"
— America, *Horse With No Name*

Tour Divide - Day 17 - 99 miles from Atlantic City, WY to Wamsutter, WY. Day 17 began with a savory food-overdose breakfast at Wild Bill's served up by Wild Bill's wife Carmella. I asked Carmella whether she is wild like Bill and she just laughed. I ate a heaping six pancakes, four strips of bacon, five scrambled eggs, three pieces of toast and a shovel full of hashed potato thingies . . . and was still hungry . . . so I ate two more pancakes coated with peanut butter. Calorie-deficient much? The day's itinerary required a crossing of the Great Divide Basin of Wyoming, consisting of hundreds of square miles of vast nothingness (oxymoronic?). Imagine Death Valley with cooler temperatures and grass dunes instead of sand dunes.

There would be no Continental Divide crossings in the Basin. In fact, what makes the Basin unique is that any rain that falls in the Basin stays in the Basin. The Basin is simply a "suckhole" in the Continental Divide that drains to neither ocean, only into itself.

Predicting the length of time to traverse the Basin is impossible. Wind speed and wind direction influence riding speed more in the Basin than anywhere else on the Tour route. With a tailwind, a rider can rip through 100 miles of the Basin in 6 hours. However, a headwind (or intolerable heat) might double or even triple that time. As there were no services or water in the Basin, I stuffed my bags with seven liters of water and over three pounds of food, an amount sufficient to last 12-14 hours. Entering the Basin, my bags did not contain a spare inch of space and my bike probably weighed over 60 pounds.

Though Atlantic City was the gateway to the Great Basin, there was no leisurely stroll through the gate. Nooooo. Wild Bill's sat at the base of steep half-mile gravel road that served as passage to the Basin. Between the heavy breakfast and the long prior day, my legs screamed, "Au contraire mon frere" (which is French for "go fuck yourself bro"), and I walked up most of the short climb.

Once in the Basin, the first ten miles passed quickly under tires and we had gleeful visions of an easy day. Now think back to proverb #23 about cockiness on the Tour. At mile ten, the road turned into a sandbox from the previous night's thunderstorm. Resistance from the soft ground made every pedal stroke a grinding sluggish chore. The only bright side was that the sandy surface did not turn into the nightmarish slop that we experienced on Banack Road back in Montana.

The trudgery continued for five miles until the ground thankfully became firm again. Phew. If the soft conditions persisted, it might have taken two days to get through the Basin.

Miles 15 to 30 weaved through blowing sagebrush and curious antelopes and led us deep into the heart of the Basin. The expansive open land provided mesmerizing views of vast raw wilderness in every direction. No mountain ranges flank the east and west boundaries of the Basin (which accounts for the crazy winds that typically blow through) and we left far behind the Wind River range that overlooked the northern edge of the Basin. Heading south, we strained to see the high peaks of Colorado, but they were beyond our line of vision at just over 100 miles away.

At mile 30, we enjoyed a ripping descent only to discover the dreaded blue line on our bike computer screens. Somehow, we missed a turn at the top of the previous sand hill. We turned around, traipsed back up the hill, and scratched our heads. Where was the trail? Apparently, the turn we missed was onto an undiscernible overgrown old jeep trail. Who mapped out this route? Obviously someone wandering the Basin in the throes of Peyote or magic mushrooms!

For the next few miles, we followed an invisible and seemingly random path over rocks and through knee-high grass while staring fixedly at the red line on our bike computers. Staying on course was a unique challenge.

At mile 40, we internally celebrated another milestone by crossing the halfway point of the Tour Divide at 1,365 miles. I say internally because we actually did not realize the achievement until we stopped for our next break. And I do not know if 'celebrated' is the right word, as there was something mildly defeating about only being halfway to the finish. Regardless, we were in no position to concern ourselves with the finish. We first had to survive this desert.

We rode a series of short slick climbs and similar short but gnarly descents before the "trail" reconnected with a dirt road at mile 45. Time for some smooth sailing right? Wrong. Without warning, my chain started skipping on my lowest gears, rendering them useless. Upon inspection, my rear cassette was loose and none of us had a tool to tighten it. This was not a huge impediment to climbing or descending. However, on the long stretches of flattish ground in the Basin, the absence of my lowest gears limited my maximum speed to 14 miles per hour. By comparison, we cranked out average sustained speeds of between 17 to 22 miles per hour on flat ground the day before.

Thanks to the cassette issue, I spent 55 miles lagging far behind my compatriots. Fortunately, our romp through the Basin occurred on a breezy and not particularly hot sunny day. With resigned acceptance, I cranked a vintage 1972 Grateful Dead show on my Bluetooth speaker and enjoyed a relaxing afternoon cruising happily and hippie-ly through the desert.

We arrived in the town of Wamsutter at 7:30PM and booked a hotel room at the half star Sagebrush Motel. Wamsutter was an exit on Interstate 80, the first of the three major transcontinental east-west interstates that crossed the Tour route. Before heading to the Sagebrush, we made a beeline for the Chester's Chicken concession at Love's Truckstop and wolfed down the nastiest fried chicken known to man. My bike chain contained less grease than the poultry. While our arteries thickened to a gooey paste, I ran into a fellow rider named Derek who passed us a few days earlier on the climb to Union Pass.

"Long day through the Basin, huh?" asked Derek as we walked outside.

"Yeah man, it was long and a little boring, but at least the weather cooperated more than my bike," I answered before explaining my cassette situation.

Derek took a quick look at my bike and said, "Well Brent, today's your lucky day as I have a tool that can fix the problem. I'm also staying at the Sagebrush. Just knock on my door after you get checked in and settled." It turned out that Derek miraculously owned a bike shop in Oregon and had miraculously spent years as a bike mechanic. Ok, maybe 'miraculous' is a bit strong on both accounts, but it was certainly fortuitous.

An hour later, Derek had fixed the cassette, but shared the disconcerting news that I had three broken spokes. Yikes. How did I miss those?

"Derek," I implored, "give me your best risk assessment for making it to Steamboat on this wheel." Steamboat Springs was 130 miles away and the next opportunity to get the bike into a shop.

"I think you'll be ok, but you should definitely try to take it easy as a series of jarring impacts on the tire could be catastrophic," Derek responded clinically.

"Catastrophic?" I nervously asked. "Please explain."

Derek elucidated, "Well, your wheel could 'taco' or blow up, but fortunately that is fairly rare for a rear wheel." In bike lingo, a wheel that 'tacos' is one where the wheel rim bends in two places from excessive force and the wheel folds up like a taco. Derek further pointed out that most of the spokes on the wheel were showing major stress and that I should have the whole wheel rebuilt (i.e., all spokes replaced) when I reached

Steamboat. The trials and tribulations of the Tour Divide never cease.

Despite the wheel and cassette issues, I went to sleep satisfied and excited. We ticked off another infamous challenge of the Tour Divide by getting through the Great Basin without succumbing to hunger, dehydration, heatstroke, trampling by a herd of feral horses, or some of the other afflictions that riders suffer in the Basin. We were only 68 miles from the Colorado border. Although I live in Maryland most of the year, Colorado has been my family's second home for over 35 years and is my favorite place on earth. I could not wait to reunite with my familiar playground and eagerly anticipated the high-altitude challenges ahead. Best of all, I received a text that morning from Lisa. She planned to meet us in Steamboat Springs. I could not wait to see her.

Can anyone see an actual trail?

Wait, there are some faint lines!

Trying to fix the cassette. Fail.

Chapter 27 – "But the Colorado rocky mountain high
I've seen it rainin' fire in the sky
The shadow from the starlight is softer than a lullabye
Rocky mountain high . . . in Colorado"
— John Denver, *Rocky Mountain High*

Tour Divide - Day 18 - 99 miles - Wamsutter, WY to summit of Watershed Divide, CO. We pushed off from Wamsutter at 7:30AM after a breakfast feast at the Hacienda Mendez Bar & Grill, the only restaurant in town. The first 30 miles south from Wamsutter consisted of a flat, soft, and potholed dirt road that cut a straight line through lifeless Wyoming prairie. A picture of the road appears in Wikipedia next to the term 'monotonous.' In short, it was a southern extension of the Great Basin, but far less scintillating. Yes, that was sarcasm. Again.

The next 33 miles wound up and around various treeless hills of stark pastoral beauty including one monster wall of a hill five miles short of the Colorado border that required a short push on foot due to a combination of steepness and loose gravel that made tire traction impossible. Once over the wall, we plummeted three miles downhill to the town of Savery, Wyoming, home of the Savery-famous Little Snake River Museum. The museum displayed a welcome sign for Tour Divide riders and provided a basement with chairs, tables and an assortment of fruits, snacks and drinks for bargain-basement prices. I swallowed six nectarines to satisfy a deepening fruit-withdrawal.

While mounting our steeds to exit the museum, I cranked John Denver's *Rocky Mountain High* on my speaker to get everyone excited for our impending Colorado border crossing. That choice elicited a few grins and one blank stare. It obviously got me jacked up as two miles out of Savery, I raced ahead of the group so that I could spend some quality time with the Colorado welcome sign. However, the only sign we got was a crummy little "Leaving Wyoming" sign. C'mon Colorado, step up your game! You are certainly generating enough tax revenues from the sale of weed to fund a sign at every border crossing!

Despite Colorado's appalling disinterest in properly welcoming us, I felt uncontained excitement about entering the state. We had ridden over 1500 miles and had survived Koko Claims, The Wall, Fleecer Ridge, the Montana monsoons, the Banack Road mud, and the Great Basin. Colorado was our second-to-last state and was poised to send us to our highest heights (literally) on the Tour.

Two miles into Colorado, we took a right turn south off the paved road and began spinning our wheels up a dusty 15-mile climb on a dirt road that meandered up a mountain valley. The climb was scenic, but the temperature skyrocketed into the 90s with no clouds and no trees to offer relief from the blazing heat. The higher we climbed, the higher Mother Nature's furnace blazed. Halfway up the climb, I looked at Wayne and moaned, "I am dying." We had already distanced ourselves in front of Vincent and Mario, and Chuck was faltering behind us as well.

Wayne gave me a pained smile (always a smile) and said, "Me too buddy. This heat is brutal."

We both put our heads down and slowly pedaled on.

Just as the odometer ticked off mile 15 of the climb (and mile 83 for the day), we rounded an elbow turn in the road and discovered nirvana in the form of the famous (famous on the Tour Divide) Brush Mountain Lodge. The Brush Mountain Lodge is a converted schoolhouse owned by an indefatigable woman named Kirsten. Kirsten and her compadres LOVE mountain bikers, particularly those riding the Divide route. Kirsten and crew tracked us as we slogged up the mountain, and welcomed us with bells ringing when we arrived. That was not a cliché. They literally greeted us with ringing bells and blasting music as we rolled to a stop in the front courtyard of the Lodge. Before even extricating our tired sweaty bodies from our bikes, Kirsten was out the door and dispensing her famous hugs. "Just drop your bikes on the ground and come on in!" she bellowed.

From the courtyard, she led us to her sun deck and immediately force-fed us with various pizzas, cold water, lemonade and beer. Upon finishing a pizza, another one magically and instantly appeared. Then another one. Then five more. The surreal reception reminded me of a scene from my 7th grade reading of Homer's *Odyssey*. In the scene, the temptress Circe lures Odysseus's weary band of travelers into her mansion and plies them with food and victuals . . . before turning them to swine and imprisoning them for a year at the mansion! I could happily spend a year at the Brush Mountain Lodge . . . just preferably not as a pig.

During the 90 minutes that we spent at the Lodge, another six or seven bikers arrived. Some were Tour riders and some were visiting for the evening from Steamboat. The same bells-and-hugs-show met each new arrival. The Brush Mountain Lodge was a heavenly, festive, and memorable place and I really wanted to stay the night. However, practicality trumped desire, as we needed to get to Steamboat early the next day for necessary bike repairs and were unsure how long the repairs might take. Wayne and Chuck actually succumbed to Kirsten's 'Siren' charms (another *Odyssey* reference) and elected to stay the night and hit the trail at 4AM. Mario,

Vincent and I were not fans of that plan.

At 6:30PM, I received three more hugs from Kirsten and then begrudgingly headed back out with Mario and Vincent. Steamboat was seven hours and one massive climb away.

The first ten miles from Brush Mountain Lodge consisted of an initial 'smack in the face' steep rise followed by a series of rolling hills through a lush verdant valley encircled by mountains front, back, left and right. Above the highest peak luminously shone a rising full moon. After ten miles, the road kicked steeply up. In diminishing daylight and falling temperatures, we climbed and climbed and kept on climbing. At mile 97.5 of the day, the trail steepened so precipitously that we dismounted and pushed our bikes up the final 1.5 miles under the glow of moonlight. Despite all of the tedious hike-a-bike sections on the Tour, this one was actually quite enjoyable and peaceful. The air was cool and refreshing, the trees faintly rustled, and the only sounds we heard were the hoots of scattered owls and the distant squeals, howls and calls of various unseen creatures.

We reached the 10,000-foot summit at 10PM and were received by a lone guy lounging tranquilly in front of his tent. Rudely pointing my headlight in his direction, we discovered our friend Derek from Union Pass and Wamsutter.

"Good to see you guys," said Derek. "I wasn't expecting late-night company at 10,000 feet!"

We exchanged a few pleasantries with Derek, set up our tents, and then crashed hard in contentment. I was super excited for the next day. For one, some of our new friends at the Brush Mountain Lodge declared that the downhill from our campsite was one of the epic descents on the Tour. However, another downhill thrill ride was of secondary importance. Lisa planned to meet us in Steamboat. That was both the thrill AND the hug that I wanted most!

Last meal in Wyoming

Last hill in Wyoming. Yes, it is as steep as it looks!

Colorado border sign — lame

Brush Mountain Lodge

The famous Kirsten

Moon over the valley

Chapter 28 – "Golden Slumbers fill your eyes, smiles awake you when you rise; sleep pretty darling do not cry, and I will sing a lullaby."
— The Beatles, *Golden Slumbers*

Prior to the Tour Divide, my wilderness experience was practically zero. In the past 25 years, I could count my collective camping nights on one hand, and my entire preparation for this race consisted of a single overnight trip 40 days before I left for Canada. Leaving Banff, I barely remembered how to correctly pitch and/or un-pitch my tent, and I was a total donkey when it came to rolling everything up tightly and fitting it into my bike bags. Accordingly, my pre-race plan was to camp when necessary, but find a mattress every chance I got.

I was incredibly fortunate to find likable mates who were also compatible bikers. Even luckier was finding guys who shared my sleep philosophy. In short, none of us were interested in camping in bad weather, none of us had anything to prove by extending rides deep into the night, and we all tacitly supported tailoring our daily ride plan to finish the day in a location with beds (particularly during the cold monsoonal days in Montana). That being said, we never pre-planned a lodging itinerary beyond 24 hours as varying weather and terrain conditions, combined with our unfamiliarity of the route as Tour rookies, made planning future days a futile exercise.

A typical morning began with a review of the route map and a determination of whether lodging options existed between 75 miles and 105 miles from our ride start. Then we would ride for four or five hours and re-evaluate the situation. If it appeared that day's ride was on track to finish between 7PM and 10PM in a location with a lodging option, then we would set the location as our end goal for the day. If we had phone service, we would search hotels at the location and make advance reservations. Only twice did we arrive in a populated area in the evening and forego beds to continue riding (Sawtelle, Idaho and Cuba, New Mexico).

During the first 12 nights of the race, I slept in a bed 10 nights, my tent once, and the floor of Butts Cabin once. Once we left Montana, we evenly split the nights between beds and ground. Not coincidentally, our departure from Montana also marked a drastic change to friendlier weather.

I shared most of my motel rooms with Wayne. Another stroke of great luck was that he was an ideal roommate. Neither of us snored, we both were very relaxed about where we tossed our stuff, and neither of us ever cared who got which bed. Having a constant roommate also benefitted the pocketbook with halved lodging expenses.

In retrospect, there were arguably two nights where we stopped too early and should have continued riding. However, what would have been the domino effect? Riding 30 miles past Butts Cabin on Day 3 may have shortened my entire Tour by two days. Conversely, I could have caught pneumonia from sleeping out in the storms that night. Similarly, riding 40 miles past Wise River to the High Country Lodge the evening of Day 11 would have saved us a day, but deprived us of valuable and needed rest.

As for lodging highlights and lowlights, the High Country Lodge in Polaris, MT and the Las Parras de Abiquiu guesthouse in Abiquiu, NM were by far the nicest accommodations I found on the Tour. I would even take Lisa to both places. The Budget Inn Express in Helena, MT and the Country Family Inn in Del Norte, CO were the worst. I would not send my dogs to either place. Honorable mentions for their amazing hospitality include the Ovando Inn in Ovando, MT and Wild Bill's in Atlantic City, WY. I am not sure how to rank Butts Cabin!

Chapter 29 – "Get out the toolbox boys,
I know you can fix things"
— Iggy Pop, *How do you Fix a Broken Part*

Tour Divide Day 19 - 53 miles from Watershed Divide, CO to Stagecoach State Park, CO. News alert — the morning air at 10,000 feet is frickin' freezing Mr. Bigglesworth! Anxious to descend to a lower elevation, we quickly packed up camp and started the day with a challenging rock-strewn ten-mile descent that required a heaping serving of focus for breakfast. Ironically, I made it through the technical sections without any problems, but within minutes of cruising out on the gravel road at the bottom of the descent, my chain snapped. This was no big deal as I intended to replace the chain in Steamboat anyway. We cruised a few more miles on rolling gravel and then arrived at the Clark General Store where Mario and Vincent were happy to satisfy their morning coffee fix and I was happy to post my daily Facebook update.

During the morning ride to Clark General Store, I hatched a plan to test the power of social media with my daily post. It costs approximately $1750 to provide a First Descents program experience to a young adult cancer survivor. Roughly 250 to 350 people followed my Tour Divide daily updates on Facebook. I opened my daily post with a plea to change two lives in the next 48 hours by helping me raise $3500 in small change (i.e., lunch money, coins under the cushions, etc.). I also asked First Descents to apply all money raised during the 48 hours to be marked for specific scholarships in the name of FOBTD (Friends of Brent Tour Divide). A $10 average donation by 350 people would get us there. I paid $28.35 for all of my food the day before, so I started the experiment with a $28.35 donation. For additional color, I asked my dear friend and First Descents' alumni Lindsay Forbes ("Smurfette") to post a comment briefly describing what the First Descents experience meant to her. Knowing Smurfette, I figured that she would post something by the time I arrived in Steamboat (or shortly thereafter).

From Clark General Store, we enjoyed a mellow mostly-downhill 25 paved miles to Steamboat Springs, arriving at the Ski Kare bike shop at 10AM. All of our bikes needed major work, mine to the tune of $400 in a rebuilt rear wheel, new chain, new front chain-ring, general tune-up, replacement gear cables, plus labor. I obviously still had the movie *Fletch* on my brain as I said to the technician, "And I'm gonna need 'bout ten quarts of anti-freeze, preferably Prestone. No, make that Quaker State." Again, blank stare. Not even a smirk. Jeez. Nobody gets me.

Interestingly, I did not need new brake pads. The technician said to me, "Dude, 1550 miles? Have you used your brakes?"

Apparently, I was only the third Tour Divider to come into their shop this summer who did not need new brake pads. So I had that going for me . . . which meant absolutely zilch.

The highlight of my day was reuniting with Lisa as I walked out of the bike shop. After the most welcome hug and kiss ever, she wasted no time pulling out a new razor and ordered, "Use it!" We took a quick drive up to my college friend Josh Kagan's house where I destroyed three disposable razors and basked in a long hot shower, emerging human again (rule violations #5 and #6?). After a tasty lunch with Lisa and Josh, I grabbed some groceries and returned to the bike-shop to check on progress. My bike was still on the operating table as of 2PM, so I took a lengthy nap in Lisa's car followed by more patient waiting. At around 3:30PM, we were all making small talk in the front of the bike shop when the following post from Smurfette hit my Facebook page:

> *"Grit. Courage. Determination. Brent Goldstein, with the love and support of his beautiful wife Lisa Goldstein, (AKA Stepmom), is just over half way through the hardest race of his life... and all to save the lives of young adults with cancer.*
>
> *Brent Goldstein helped SAVE MY LIFE. Beaten down by cancer, I arrived at First Descents struggling to understand a new sense of normal. Life was different now. Life was filled with the insecurities that revolve around a cancer diagnosis. Was my body strong enough and my mind powerful enough to get through everything I had to face? Would I be on this earth long enough to marry my best friend and grow old with him? Would I be here in 10 years to experience the birth of my children? No one could give me the answer to those questions, but what First Descents did give me was the strength and courage to face adversity and look toward my new normal with hope, laughter, and an incredible new family.*
>
> *This man was at my very first week with First Descents and we became instant family. There are no words to explain the overwhelming connection that is felt the minute you meet someone at FD. Love, understanding, acceptance, and a mutual agreement of "F Cancer."*

> *This man came to First Descents camp possibly more nervous than the rest of us. But it didn't show. He was quiet and we were not sure of his story, but Lord knows, we were all there with our own story to tell when we were ready.*
> *This man has a heart like no other. After a few days on the river and ranch together, we heard the story weighing on his heart and why he came to join us that summer.*
> *This man has raised over ONE MILLION DOLLARS to support cancer survivors like myself and allow them to experience the life changing power of adventure.*
> *This man and his amazing family have been my family now for almost 10 years (WHAT?!). My husband Jonathan Forbes also knows of Brent Goldstein's incredible heart has been fortunate to take part in a First Descents week dedicated to caregivers thanks to Brent.*
> *This man just passed the halfway point of the Tour Divide - a self-supported, ultra-cycling challenge from Canada to Mexico. He is doing this crazy, grueling race all in the name of First Descents. I invite you to follow his story through the link below and donate to his race in support of him and the lives, like mine, that he is forever saving.*
> *This man is incredible. We love you Brent Goldstein*

As I read these beautiful words, my emotions swelled beyond their bursting point and my tear ducts exploded in the middle of the bike shop. Nobody, including Lisa, knew what the hell was going on with me. Tears cascaded down my face and onto the floor. I could only hand Lisa my phone and let her read what I had just read. Her eyes moistened and she handed the phone to Wayne, who read the post and then nodded in understanding. It was a powerful and poignant moment and my complete and public loss of composure was a bit embarrassing. After a few minutes and a few wet sleeves, I got myself back together.

My bike was finally ready at 4PM along with Mario's and Vincent's bikes, but Wayne's bike still needed work. Mario pulled me aside and asked, "Brent, what are you thinking?" I could tell that he and Vincent were antsy to get out of there, but felt badly about leaving Wayne. I think the cumulative fatigue was also hitting Vincent a little harder than the rest of us and Mario figured that it might be advantageous to get out ahead and let us eventually catch them.

"Mario," I responded, "why don't you guys take off? I am happy to hang with Lisa a bit longer and am ok waiting around for Wayne. I think Chuck is in no hurry to head out yet either, so we are good. We'll catch you either later this evening or sometime tomorrow."

After a 7-day spree averaging 100 miles a day, I was also fine with a few more hours of rest.

Thirty minutes after Mario and Vincent left, we learned that Wayne's bike required a part for his front shifter carried by neither Ski Kare, nor any other shop in Steamboat. It got worse. After multiple phone calls and internet searches, it appeared that no shop within 200 miles of Steamboat carried the part. Now what? As a last resort, Mike, the main technician at Ski Kare, remembered that a local Steamboat customer owned the same bike as Wayne and maybe the guy would give Wayne the part and Wayne would in turn replace it with a new one. However, as this was the Tour Divide and no solution should be too easy, we learned that the customer was traveling in Europe. Although it was after midnight in Europe, Mike somehow magically tracked the guy down by phone and obtained instructions for getting into his garage and retrieving the part. So Lisa and I went and enjoyed a relaxing dinner in town while Wayne commandeered Lisa's car, drove to the guy's house, grabbed the part, brought it back to Mike, and Mike and his crew stayed late to install the part and get Wayne's bike ready to roll. I have no idea how much money and beer Wayne promised those guys to make that happen!

In the meantime, Lisa was planning to meet us again in Silverthorne, Colorado the following evening and had a two-hour drive back to Avon, so I sent her on her way after dinner. Wayne's bike was finally ready at 8:15PM, and Chuck, Wayne and I took off from Steamboat under darkening but clear starry skies. We briefly considered staying in Steamboat, but we were restless from loitering around the bike-shop all day and were determined to eat up some of the 113 miles from Steamboat to Silverthorne to ease the next day's burden.

We rode 18 miles into the night, the last four miles consisting of a low-gradient climb up a quiet mountain dirt road, before stumbling upon the entrance of Stagecoach State Park and setting up camp in the empty parking area. Without a hint of clouds in the sky, I did not bother attaching my tent fly cover to the tent and fell asleep counting the billion stars directly overhead.

Good morning from 10,000 feet!

Ramshackle or rustic? You decide.

Pit-stop on way down to Steamboat.

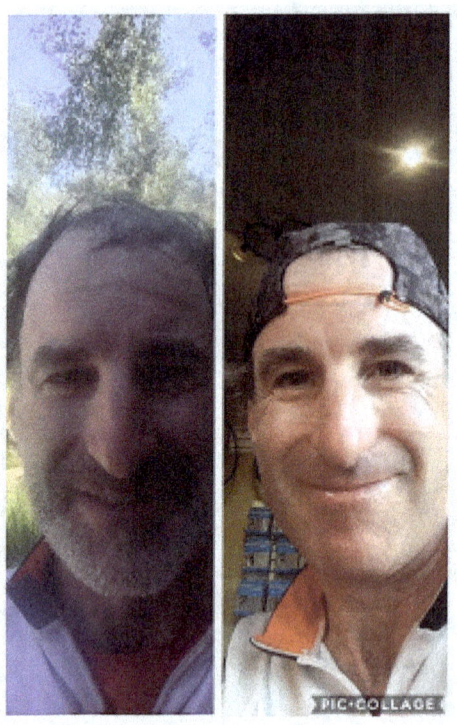

Before   After

Chapter 30 – "I see skies of blue and clouds of white
The bright blessed day, the dark sacred night
And I think to myself what a wonderful world"
— Louis Armstrong, *It's a Wonderful World*

Tour Divide Day 20 - 107.2 miles from Stagecoach State Park, CO to Silverthorne, CO - 9,000+ feet of climbing. A bright sunrise interrupted a blissful night of sleep and we were back on the bikes by 7AM (Chuck took off 45 minutes before us). Our first pedal revolutions of the day propelled us up a well-maintained gravel path that ascended to a placid mountain lake dotted by a scattered assortment of colorful houses and docks along the shoreline. The scene looked more reminiscent of something from a Norwegian travel brochure than Colorado. The path circled half the perimeter of the lake before turning east onto a narrow valley dirt road that gently climbed toward Lynx Pass. The first ten miles of the road rolled through several large ranches before steepening in the final miles approaching the pass.

I typically play energizing music for climbs. For this cool tranquil morning, I slowed things down with a playlist of mellow acoustic cover songs. During a 30-minute stretch leading to Lynx Pass, everything came together for me. It was a gorgeous sunny morning, I was in my favorite mountains (Colorado), every turn in the road provided a postcard view, and I was on a pristine trail doing something I love. I felt pure contentment. I was unaware of the date or the day of the week and three weeks into a news and politics blackout. I had no calls or messages to return, carpools to run, or meetings to attend. Other than following the red line, I had nowhere to be and was in no hurry to get there. For the first time in weeks, all of my physical maladies as well as my self-doubts, fears and concerns melted away. THIS is what the Tour Divide was all about. THIS is what adventure was all about. THIS is what life should be about. Finding joy. Of course, joy through adventure does not require an insane 2700-mile bike race. It can come through simple escape. For me, however, joy is magnified by escapes to realms beyond my comfort zone.

As I crested Lynx Pass, the late Eva Cassidy's sublime cover of Louie Armstrong's *It's a Wonderful World* emanated from my speaker. It was perfect. At the pass, there was another picturesque lake and we stopped for a few minutes to take in the quiet beauty. On cue, we got a double-dose of Eva Cassidy as *Wonderful World* morphed into a cover of John Lennon's *Imagine*. For those not familiar with Eva Cassidy, she was a singer-songwriter with an angelic voice who tragically died of cancer in 1996 at the tender age of 33. Few artists could conjure emotion like Eva Cassidy.

Amazingly, the next 15-20 miles after Lynx Pass got even better as we gleefully traversed a lightly travelled roller-coaster trail through the southern portion of the Bow-Routt National forest. This trail flowed up and down and twisted back and forth through switchbacks, hairpins and horseshoes, culminating with an exhilarating and harrowing five-mile descent to a campground on the Colorado River in a village called Radium. I reached the campground 15 minutes before Wayne and Chuck (we caught up to Chuck a mile before the descent). With the temperature heating into the 90s, I used that 15 minutes to remove my shoes and socks and eat, you guessed it, a burrito, while submerging my feet in the river.

So far, this was my favorite day on the Tour Divide.

While finishing lunch, I received a text from Lisa notifying me that a crew of friends wanted to meet me for dinner in Silverthorne, CO at 7:30PM. It was 1:30PM as I took my last bite of food and we still had some 58 miles and two huge climbs to go. I calculated several scenarios in my head and determined that the only way I would make it to dinner on time was by taking off alone and riding those 58 miles at a race-pace with minimal stops. Wayne and Chuck gave me their best "have at it" salutes and I was gone.

Feeling refreshed after the lunch break, I hammered the first climb out of Radium. Unfortunately, I then began to wilt from the blisteringly hot cloudless day and a 40-mile stretch with no shady relief. I carried plenty of water following the discovery of a water hose in Radium, but I craved a cold soda as a pick-me-up.

At mile 50, I had the option of diverting to the town of Kremmling to grab food, soda and shade. Regrettably, Kremmling was two miles off the route and I did not have the time to spare to make it punctually to dinner. Onward ho.

While circling a large lake (which I later learned was called the Williams Fork Reservoir) at mile 65, a car pulled up next to me blasting the song *Eye of the Tiger* through open windows. With a wry smile, I slowly gazed left and was amused to see an SUV carrying my friends Ray Shedd, Andrew Coulter and Emma Burick from First Descents. They screamed, I screamed (we all screamed for ice cream). What a sight for sore dry eyes. They drove alongside me for four miles of relatively flat terrain and took some great pictures and video before letting me return to my overheated pain-cave.

At 6:10PM, the dirt road began tilting skyward as I began the last climb of the day toward Ute Pass. About halfway up the climb, I caught Mario and Vincent.

Pulling alongside them, I said, "What's up guys? Nice day for a hot bike ride!"

Vincent looked up and responded, "Heeeey, where did you come from? You were 25 miles back at last check. And yes, it is damn hot out here. I'm struggling a bit."

I let them know that Wayne and Chuck were together, but probably a good hour or more behind me and shared with them our plans for the evening to stay in Silverthorne. Mario said that they would probably continue beyond Silverthorne for the next town of Frisco. I said that we would hopefully catch them in the next few days and then I sped ahead.

As I crested Ute Pass, a lone rider on a road-bike approached from the other direction and said, "Are you Brent?"

Somewhat confused, I responded, "Uh, yes. Who are you?"

The rider replied, "I'm Dan. I'm friends with Wayne. I've been tracking you guys and came out to ride the last few miles with you. Where the hell is Wayne?"

I told Dan that I was racing to get to Silverthorne to meet friends and that Wayne and Chuck had to be a good 20+ miles behind me.

Dan said, "Right on brother, I'll go find 'em" and we continued in opposite directions.

After Ute Pass, I was confident that I would make it to Silverthorne by 7:15PM as I only had five miles to go. Or so I thought. The section from Steamboat to Silverthorne was supposed to be 113 miles. We covered 18 miles the night before and thus should have had 95 miles in total today. Believe me, I am quite proficient at simple arithmetic. I was therefore not amused when my odometer hit 96 miles on the descent from Ute Pass. As I descended, 96 became 98 which became 100 and Silverthorne was nowhere in sight. Worst of all, the road then turned slightly acclivous (thank you for that word Peter Mark Roget!).

7:15PM came and went. So did miles 101, 102 and 103. By then I was exhausted, starving and aggravated. Then it was 7:30PM and the miles still accumulated. 104, 105, 106.

I finally reached the hotel and Lisa in Silverthorne at 7:45PM after 107 hot miles and over 9,000 feet of climbing. It was a fantastic day, but I did not need the bonus miles. I am not sure how we got mistaken mileage intel.

I quickly threw my stuff in the room, showered, and headed to the restaurant to celebrate 1,684 miles with a group consisting of local Colorado friends and D.C. area friends visiting Colorado. My friends stared at me with bemusement as I devoured a plate of onion rings followed by two full entrees and a supersized chocolate milkshake! It was a great end to a memorable day.

Endnotes to the day: Mario and Vincent bypassed Silverthorne and made it to Frisco. Wayne and Chuck arrived in Silverthorne at 10:15PM and grabbed a room at my motel. Additionally, a momentous milestone was reached at mile 96 of the day as that marked 1,000 miles to the race finish. During those unwanted bonus miles into Silverthorne, I calculated that if we could average just under 100 miles a day from this point forward, we could actually finish the race on Day 30 (July 7). However, as I exhaustedly went to sleep that night, I could not fathom how I was going to wake up the next day and ride 100 miles after that day's 6+ hours of non-stop race-pace. I was hoping for my 65th second wind of the Tour Divide!

Stagecoach State Park - parking lot/camp

Morning lake

Bow-Routt National Forest

Up up and away

Happiness in my Colorado playground

It was worth killing myself for these folks!

Chapter 31 – "O give me a home where the buffaloes roam
Where the deer and the antelope play
Where seldom is heard a discouraging word
And the skies are not cloudy all day"
— Bing Crosby, *Home on the Range*

Tour Divide Day 21 - 78 miles - Silverthorne, CO to an abandoned roofless prairie shack on the side of a dirt road south of Hartsel, CO. The Day 20 ride from Stagecoach State Park to Silverthorne was my favorite day on the Tour Divide. The morning ride was memorable and rhapsodic and finishing the day over dinner with Lisa and friends in Silverthorne was emotionally uplifting. However, Tour Divide highs often quickly give way to Tour Divide lows. Race pacing the last 65 miles in the blistering 95-degree sun to get to Silverthorne for dinner wrecked me.

My summer of discomfiting emotion continued with a tearful goodbye to Lisa. I would see her again in less than ten days, but emotions intensify under stress, and the stress of the Tour was beyond expectation. Fortunately, a special surprise awaited at breakfast. Within minutes of taking our seats at the Morning Lyon Café in Silverthorne, my friends Larry and Kim Weinberg pulled up to the restaurant in their car. Larry and Kim left McLean, Virginia, destination Vail, not long after Wayne and I pulled out of the Stagecoach parking lot early the prior morning. They drove all day and all night across the heartland of the United States just so they could surprise me for breakfast. Thanks to Lisa for pulling the logistical strings. It was awesome to see them and their marathon driving effort touched me deeply. And just as I awed my friends the night before by the ridiculous amount of food consumed at dinner, Larry and Kim were equally stunned and amused by the massive breakfasts that Wayne and I shoveled down at the Mountain Lyon (Chuck headed out early and would meet us down the trail).

As we were saying our farewells to Kim and Larry in the Mountain Lyon parking lot, Wayne's friend Dan (from the day before) rode up on a mountain bike and said "good morning gentlemen! Allow me to escort you to Boreas Pass!" The more the merrier.

From the parking lot, our ride started with a steep set of switchbacks that took us from Silverthorne to the Lake Dillon bike-path 150 feet above town. We circled the lake past the town of Frisco, where we stopped at a traffic light at the main intersection of town. While waiting for the light to turn green, I hesitated with the realization that a right turn at the light instead of left would lead me to my couch in Avon in under three hours!

Fortunately, it was only a fleeting thought and when the light turned green, I turned left toward Breckenridge.

The route from Frisco to Breckenridge was on a crowded public bike path that ascended gently the whole way. Between lingering exhaustion from the prior day, the uphill grade of the bike path, and a developing headwind, I could not get anything going. My legs felt like Jell-O pudding and the needle on my enthusiasm gauge was hovering near empty.

A few miles from Breckenridge, my friend Matt "Mateo" Hayne and his lovely girlfriend-now-fiancée Emily (aka "Hot Heat") joined us on the path and escorted us into town. Mateo is a two-time cancer survivor, a First Descents alum and a former First Descents program leader who now lives in Breckenridge. He also raced the Leadville 100 with me in 2011 and 2012. We briefly stopped at a bike-shop and grocery in town for a quick gearing adjustment and some supplies, before departing Breckenridge for an 1800-foot climb up to Boreas Pass at 11,450 feet. Thankfully, it was a smooth low-gradient climb with nonstop visual distractions including a stunning view of a valley floor lake called Goose Pasture Tarn. More importantly, the moderate incline was a tonic for my weary legs. Finally, having Dan and Mateo as new conversants also made the climb pass enjoyably.

At Boreas Pass, we stopped for obligatory pictures at the Continental Divide sign and reviewed the trail map. In addition to famous landmarks on the Tour Divide, Tour Lore also includes several infamous easy-to-miss turns. The Gold Rush Trail descends from Boreas Pass and is marked by an inconspicuous trailhead located 100 yards below the pass. Tour Lore offers countless stories about riders who miss this turn and descend two or three miles below the pass before discovering their mistake and frustratingly climbing back up. As a local, Dan was well aware of the Gold Rush Trail and chaperoned us to the turn-off.

The Gold Rush Trail was a blast. It began as an exposed stretch of technical single-track that descended steeply and crossed two creeks on old sketchy wood bridges. The trail then dropped into an old drainage ditch that some hard-working mountain bikers turned into a veritable bobsled run for mountain bikes with bermed curves and raised banks on both sides of the trail. This blissfully continued for several miles until the trail spit us out on a gravel road that dropped into the one-horse village of Como at mile 37.

Then everything fell apart.

The next section after Como consisted of a smooth and easy 76 miles to the town of Salida where we would find beds for the night and dinner from a pick of a handful of craft breweries. Someone did not get that

memo. Almost immediately after leaving Como, nasty whipping sustained headwinds of 25 to 35 miles per hour blew dust and dirt into our faces, reduced forward progress to a crawl, made flat ground seem like climbing a steep ascent, and made conversation impossible. To illustrate, I attempted the following conversation with Wayne an hour after leaving Como:
    Me: "I think we still have 16 miles to go on this dirt road."
    Wayne: "What?"
    Me, talking louder: "I think we still have 16 miles to go on this dirt road."
    Wayne: "What?"
    Me, screaming: "I THINK WE STILL HAVE 16 FUCKING MILES TO GO ON THIS FUCKING DIRT ROAD!"
    Wayne: "What? You think I look like a fucking toad?"
    Me: Sigh

It was relentless and miserable and it took us four hours to go a mere 32 miles on otherwise benign terrain. As a point of comparison, on our 130-mile jaunt through the Wind River Valley the prior Saturday, the tailwinds escorted us 32 miles on comparable terrain in 90 minutes.

Despite all attempts to "live in the moment" and "peacefully accept whatever the elements throw at us," we arrived in the town of Hartsel, CO at mile 67 at 6:15PM physically worn out and mentally defeated. We entered the Highline Cafe (the only restaurant in town) and I wanted to crawl under a table and pass out on the ceramic tiled floor. We sat down, ordered food, and looked at the maps to figure out our options. Salida was 46 miles away. With the south-wind from hell, that was out. The route between Hartsel and Salida primarily consisted of more open windswept prairie with zero lodging options and zero noted camping options. Hartsel was likewise bereft of lodging options, so there was no point calling it quits there.

Chuck declared, "It is time to break out the big artillery." He then summoned the waitress and ordered a Vanilla milkshake. Wayne went for Strawberry. I completed the milkshake rainbow with Chocolate. The milkshakes provided temporary rejuvenation. Thank you Highline Cafe!

With our spirits slightly buoyed by frozen dairy goodness, we pulled out of Hartsel at 7:30PM aiming to ride another hour or two. Our hope was to camp in a ditch or set of trees that would block the wind just enough to prevent our tents from blowing back to Wyoming. We made it ten miles with neither a ditch, nor any trees in sight. Just as the sun set over the mountains to our west and we resigned ourselves to riding deep into the night, we spied a distant old wooden log cabin situated 100 yards west of the dirt road. Nearing, we noticed that the cabin lacked a roof, but it had four walls that would provide a suitable shelter from the wind.

   We cautiously approached the north door of the structure, peered inside, and were relieved to find no human or animal squatters. The cabin's floor disintegrated eons ago, leaving a sandy surface covered with sagebrush and several calcified cow-pies. Peering at Wayne, I remarked, "With some new drapes, this cabin would be at least three and a half stars better than the Budget Inn Express in Helena!" Wayne cracked up and readily agreed.

   We quickly brought our bikes inside, tossed the cow-pies out the cabin doorways, cleared the sagebrush, set up our tents, and turned off all headlamps so no passing cars would see us (as there was a sign in front that said "Private Property - No Trespassing").

   Before falling asleep to the unsettling sounds of the howling wind, I typed up my daily blog and thought about the last 14 hours. I knew the crushed legs from yesterday's massive effort would make today a formidable challenge. However, there is a difference between challenge borne from weariness versus challenge derived from weather conditions. I have had plenty of experience riding in brutal headwinds, but usually it is only for an hour or two, and usually in places where there are trees or hills or structures or changes of direction that provide relief from the wind. I had never before encountered six straight hours of fierce exposed direct headwinds. It was not as abusive as the rocks of Koko Claims or the mud of Bannack Road, but it was still miserable in a way that defies description.

   I had no choice but to set today aside and hope for a better tomorrow. Additionally, I hoped that the Tour's bag of evil tricks was now empty as we had faced, in no particular order: snow, hail, torrential rain, freezing temperatures, swarming mosquitos, blistering heat, avalanche debris, hellacious hike-a-bike sections, horrendous peanut-buttery mud, and ferocious headwinds. What was left? Little did we know that the weather pattern over the southwest dramatically changed in the prior 24 hours and this day marked the first day of a three-week stretch of unending brisk winds shooting straight north from Mexico that no border wall could restrain.

View from road to Boreas Pass

Boreas Pass with Wayne and Chuck

Boreas Pass with Mateo

Gold Rush Trail

Oops, Wayne put his foot down!

Chuck kept his feet on the pedals

More Gold Rush Trail

Prairie road into ferocious headwind

Hark . . . lodging on the horizon

Needs some curtains, but it will do.

Moldy carpeting

Chapter 32– "The hills are alive with the sound of music
With songs they have sung for a thousand years
The hills fill my heart with the sound of music
My heart wants to sing every song it hears"
— Julie Andrews, *The Sound of Music*

During and after the Tour, countless friends asked me how I managed boredom and how I kept my mind fruitfully occupied day after long day for a month. My answer is one word: MUSIC. I spend 90% of the waking hours of my life listening to music. I work with music, read with music, drive with music, relax with music, and recreate with music. Most memories of my life are associated with a song, a soundtrack, or an album. I cannot play an instrument for shit, but I remember every word of the Beatles' *White Album* and Bob Dylan's *Blood on the Tracks* from the days when albums were a thing. By design, every chapter in this book is preceded by song lyrics that are either relevant to the chapter or that popped up on a playlist that day on the Tour.

When I committed to race the Tour Divide, my first purchase was the JBL Bluetooth speaker. Earphones have been my audio conduit of choice for most of my biking life. However, I thought it would be safer on the Tour to blare tunes from the handlebars instead of earphones so that I could hear things around me . . . such as the sound of a charging bull moose. In addition, 85%-90% of the route was off-road, so competing car and truck noise would be minimal.

In early January, my daughters introduced me to Spotify. What a game-changer! Every song in the world not sung by Garth Brooks or Taylor Swift was at my fingertips. It was time to dust off the playlist "mix-tape" skills I developed in college and get to work producing playlists for the Tour Divide.

I decided to have some fun with my music project. In late January, I submitted a post on Facebook asking friends to share songs that made them happy and/or smile. No boundaries. I collected over 230 songs and spent a week listening to snippets of every one (many of which I recognized neither the song, nor the artist). The result of that work was my first Tour Divide playlist that I aptly titled "Happy Friends."

As a joke, one of my smart-ass friends (Jonathan Forbes) responded to the happy tunes request with "any Disney tune." I briefly laughed and then realized that he was on to something. Who does not smile when they hear Disney songs? With the magic of Spotify, I created a "Showtunes" playlist consisting of 258 songs from movies and plays, including many old Disney favorites. Hi ho!

The Showtunes playlist led to a related "Movie Soundtracks" playlist consisting of nearly 300 instrumental songs from movie soundtracks. I was unsure where or when I might listen to that kind of music on the Divide, but wanted it available if the right moment arose.

I tossed out a few more concept post requests on Facebook and, in the months leading up to my departure, built a diverse library of playlists. I had playlists based on themes such as songs with numbers in the titles (i.e., *8 Days a Week* or *7 Bridges Road*) or songs with places in the titles (i.e., *Sweet Home Chicago* or *California Dreamin*). I made playlists based on genres such as reggae and new age. I made playlists of just John Denver songs, just Grateful Dead live songs and just Beatles songs. I made a "crooners" playlist, an "acoustic covers" playlist, a "dead rockers" playlist, a "rock-out" playlist, two mellow playlists (one mellower than the other), a "classical anthems" playlist, and a "songs-that-evoke-personal-memories" playlist. By the time I left for Canada, I had enough music to fill 30 days of 12-hour rides.

Ultimately, the playlist that got the most 'play' on the Tour Divide was a playlist aptly entitled "Going Deep –Tour Divide." During reflective moments in the days and months preceding the Tour, I vividly envisioned majestic snow-capped mountains at sunrise or sunset, often with ominous clouds and richly colored sky hues. I pictured myself riding at the base of these mountains and imagined the music that would enhance the scene. It was always music with depth, soul, and meaning, and often with dark or heavy overtones. I assembled a playlist with about 140 of these songs and played that playlist at least ten times throughout the Tour . . . especially in the many places where the visual reality merged with my imagined perceptions. As everyone has a different interpretation of what is soulful, a sample list of songs on this playlist is probably more illuminating than my attempted description:

Dream On – Aerosmith
Soulshine – Allman Brothers
God Only Knows – Beach Boys
Black Diamond Bay – Bob Dylan
Who the Cap Fit – Bob Marley
Don't Panic – Coldplay
Perfect Blue Buildings – Counting Crows
The Lee Shore – CSN&Y

Cortez the Killer – Neil Young
Youth - Daughter
Riders on the Storm – The Doors
Wasted Time – The Eagles
My Silver Lining – First Aid Kit
Let it Grow – Grateful Dead
Looking For Space – John Denver
Crossing Muddy Waters – John Hiatt
Battle of Evermore – Led Zeppelin
Tuesday's Gone – Lynyrd Skynyrd
Fragile – Sting
Black – Pearl Jam
Comfortably Numb – Pink Floyd
Half a World Away – REM
Monkey Man – Rolling Stones
Red Barchetta – Rush
It's Good to be King – Tom Petty
Sweet Thing – Van Morrison

My other go-to for any long stretch of riding were Grateful Dead shows. Prior to the Tour, I downloaded 30 Dead shows onto my iPhone attempting to cover most of the years between 1969 and Jerry Garcia's death in 1995. I probably listened to 20 of the 30 shows, including one 1976 show from Shrine Auditorium in Los Angeles that I played three different times.

Chapter 33 – "Oh you got to learn to roll with the changes
Got to, got to, got to, got to keep on rollin'
Keep on rollin', got to learn to, got to learn to,
Got to learn to roll"
— REO Speedwagon, *Roll With the Changes*

Tour Divide Day 22 - 79 miles from prairie cabin south of Hartsel, CO to Sargents, CO. After a decent night's sleep in the roofless Ritz-Carlton, the first morning of the fourth week on the Tour Divide welcomed us with bright sunshine and the same loathsome headwind that put us to bed the night before. With nothing left to do but smile, smile, smile, we laced up our boxing gloves, hit the dirt road at 7AM and resumed our Battle of the Breeze for 28 miles to Salida, CO.

At mile 16 we started a lengthy climb into the San Isabel National Forest that summited an unnamed pass that offered mouth-gaping views of the southern Sawatch Mountain range and several distant 14ers (Mt. Antero and Mt. Princeton). I was actually thankful for the climb, as I preferred climbing into the wind to riding flat roads in the wind (it is a mental thing). Following the pass, we cruised for nine miles down one of the more glorious descents of the Tour Divide, dropping 3,000 feet on a well-maintained dirt road that deposited us on the edge Salida. Fun irrelevant fact: in 2017, *Outside Magazine* named Salida as the Best Unsung Mountain Town in the United States.

In Salida, we headed straight to the local bike shop (Absolute Bikes) for repairs (my brake pads finally needed replacing) followed by a relaxing lunch at a Mexican restaurant overlooking the Arkansas River. The last 36 hours spent fighting the wind sapped our enthusiasm for heading back out after lunch, especially with a temperature in the mid-90s and an immediate future containing a 25-mile 4,000 foot climb.

After lunch, we walked back along the river toward the bike shop and bumped into the Sheilas. We were quite puzzled by this chance encounter as we had been tracking them off and on since Montana and knew them to be at least two days behind us.

Wayne asked Austin Sheila, "How in the world did you both get here so fast?"

Austin Sheila responded, "We called it quits yesterday and caught a ride to Salida where we are meeting a friend to drive us back to Texas."

They did not really seem too interested in elaborating on why they called it quits, so we idly chatted for another minute or so, they wished us luck and we said farewell.

The first few miles out of Salida were on a bike-path with a slight uphill grade artificially steepened by . . . drumroll . . . headwinds. Four miles from Salida, we passed through the town of Poncha Springs and began a five-mile, 1200-foot climb on the thin gravelly shoulder of a busy four-lane highway. The next 45 minutes on that highway was a Tour Divide lowlight. Trucks passed within mere feet of us, the temperature hit 98 degrees, the incline was a steep eight percent to nine percent, and the wind, a wind that felt like it was blowing from a hot oversized furnace fan, was once again in our faces.

Many comments on my Facebook posts over the prior few days had mentioned admiration for my determination and will. I appreciated the sentiments, but my will was anything but indomitable. Will is easy when there is reason and purpose to serve it. Aside from wanting to do something epic to celebrate my 50th birthday, I was racing the Tour to raise a lot of money for a cause near and dear to me, and in memory of my late pal Allan Goldberg. Take away either or both of those two incentives and I likely would have quit this silly race five different times by Day 22. Riding up the shoulder of that stinkin' highway was another one of those times. Halfway up, I wanted nothing more than to turn around, cruise back to Salida, lie down in the Arkansas River, and then go home to a couch. Then I thought of all those battling cancer for whom quitting is not an option. I thought of Allan who could not pronounce the word 'quit.' I thought of my wife and daughters who sacrificed so I could do this race. After administering a dose of self-admonishment, I kept pedaling and awaiting change . . . change in terrain, change in weather, change in attitude, all of the above.

Thank Zeus, change arrived quickly when we turned off the highway. The next 16 miles climbed a forested dirt road with a consistent moderate grade of two percent to three percent. Best of all, the temperature dramatically dropped once we ascended into the mountains and away from the highway. The climb also twisted and turned in so many different directions that we never had to confront the crazy headwind for more than a few minutes at a time.

The higher we climbed, the better the views. At one point, we looked down on a hidden lake (O'Haver Lake) that has probably graced the cover of some outdoor magazine. Tall Ponderosa pines, Aspen trees, and colorful tents surrounded the lake and the clear water surface provided a vivid reflection of the mountains soaring above the trees behind the lake. This was one of the few times on the Tour Divide where I chose not to take a picture and simply took an indelibly etched snapshot in my mind.

The climb reached its acme at a convergence of landmarks consisting of the Marshall Pass, the Continental Divide and the Colorado Trail. This was our 17th or 18th crossing of the Divide. I lost track. From the pass, we flew down a spine-tingling 18-mile descent into the village of Sargents where we rented a cabin, inhaled dinner and turned in early. Over dinner, we determined that the nasty winds of the last two days had cost us some 40-50 miles and half a day. Worse, the winds were compounding our cumulative physical and mental fatigue. My gas tank was empty and my engine was running on fumes.

During my evening pre-sleep reflections, I excoriated myself for letting the wind so negatively affect my mood at times. For whatever reason, I was unable to locate the mental switch that could change my mood with a simple flick. As an aside, the owner of the cabin-park told us that high wind advisories were in effect all over Colorado and would likely continue for another week. We were just unlucky to be going in the wrong direction at the wrong time. Once again, I shut my eyes telling myself that tomorrow is a new day. We had 883 miles to go.

Morning departure from the "Resort"

The Long and winding (and windy) road

San Isabel National Forest

Marshall Pass

Descent from Marshall Pass

Setting sun in haze

Chapter 34 - "Roll out those lazy, hazy, crazy days of summer
Those days of soda and pretzels and beer
Roll out those lazy, hazy, crazy days of summer
You'll wish that summer could always be here"
— Nat King Cole, *Lazy, Hazy Crazy Days of Summer*

Tour Divide Day 23 - 113 miles from Sargents, CO to Del Norte, CO. After two frustrating and demoralizing days fighting a Battle Royale against the Wicked Witch of Headwinds, we left Sargents at 6AM aiming to ride 113 miles to the town of Del Norte. The first 13 miles were on pavement and, holy crap, the wind was at our backs! Hallefuckingllujah! We covered the 13 miles in 45 minutes and had frozen fingers and toes when we turned onto the dirt, as it was a nipply 33 degrees. No matter. I'll take the cold after frying in the heat the day before.

Once the sun rose over the mountains, the morning air heated up nicely and we had a perfect 15 miles of {insert synonym for "beautiful" adjective here} rolling prairie followed by a mellow 17-mile climb into the Rio Grande Nat'l Park and up to Cochetopa Pass on the Continental Divide (confirmed as our 18th crossing). Halfway up the climb, it dawned on me that my left Achilles tendon was not sore for the first time since Day 4. Comically, I rode for two weeks (since Bannack Road in Montana) with one flat pedal (left) and one clipless pedal (right). It was time to take a little risk. I swapped the flat left pedal with my clipless left pedal and started slowly with a few easy pedal strokes. No pain. I then stood up on the pedals for five straight minutes and still felt no pain. I finished the climb rotating between sitting and standing and the tendon felt great. So far so good. We covered 45 miles in just over four hours, I had no pain from the matching clipless pedals, and there was no hint of wind . . . yet.

After a fast downhill from Cochetopa and a five-mile pavement connector, we re-entered the Rio Grande Nat'l Park at mile 63. It was starting to get hot and I felt sluggish, so I hit shuffle on my "Happy Friends" music playlist, forced my lips to widen into a smile, and then climbed ten happy miles and 1700 happy feet to Carnero Pass, arriving at 2:30PM. Thanks friends!

Unfortunately, despite their cool "C" names, neither of the two passes had any great views at the top. Just non-descript signs in the woods.

From Carnero Pass, we faced a bi-polar 18-mile descent. I say bi-polar because the first ten miles were fast, smooth and joyous, but the last eight miles were akin to riding in a gravel sandbox. A few chapters ago, I wondered whether the Tour Divide could play any more tricks on us. Well, JACKPOT, there was one more thing! It is a nasty little asshole called "washboard." Washboard is a phenomenon that happens to dirt and gravel roads when a pattern of ripples forms across the roads from weather or vehicle treads. If the ripples are solid, it is annoying but a mountain bike can maintain speed through it. However, when the ripples are soft, a bike can literally ground to a halt or skid out. We experienced sections of washboard over the first 22 days, but none was particularly noteworthy.

The last eight miles of the Carnero descent won the ignominious award for being the Mother of all Washboards. When not grinding to a stop, we bounced around until it felt as if our teeth would disengage from our gums and leap from our mouths. Despite immense frustration, I laughed. This was just another stall at the Tour Divide carnival and, once again, there would be no cute furry participation prizes.

We finally exited the washboard at mile 93. It was 4:30PM and we had only 20 miles to Del Norte. This was great! We would get to Del Norte by around 6PM and actually have some time to kick back and relax. Oh but wait you silly boy! There is NO relaxing on the Tour Divide! The route took a hard turn to the west and we hit the trifecta of misery: crazy west-wind plus sandboxy road plus washboard the size of small waves on an angry lake. I screamed aloud, "FU Tour Divide!"

The Tour Divide just snickered and flipped me the bird.

The soft gravel road thankfully turned to dirt after four miles and climbed north back into the Rio Grand Nat'l Park. The dirt climb was far preferable to the flat soft gravel. At least when climbing, there is no expectation of fast progress. As I said in a prior chapter, it is a mental thing. At the top of the climb, the trail narrowed and turned into several entertaining miles of flowy double-track with swoops and drops and berms and views and sand and sugar and spice and everything nice. This section is where Matthew Lee wiped out in the *Ride the Divide* movie. I imagined that there were countless biker yard sales on this descent ("yard sale" being defined as a horrendous crash that leaves all your various "wares" — water bottles, pump, tool bag, etc. — scattered on the ground as if on display for sale) as some of the turns were banked with several inches of soft sand that no tire tread could grip. I carried enough speed to remain perpendicular to the ground the whole way down, but Wayne and Chuck were not so lucky behind me as they each enjoyed dining on some unsalted sagebrush snacks during their descents. Fortunately, the soft sand meant soft landings!

After some derisive laughter (on my part) and frustration (on Wayne's and Chuck's parts), the fun double-track descent dropped us onto a flattish dirt road that would take us the last five miles into Del Norte. Mama Nature must have been annoyed that we found amusement in her sand park and decided to really mess with us on the final stretch into Del Norte. Suddenly the wind kicked up three notches from brisk to Kansas. Mini dust funnels kicked up on the road all around us and a full-on raging dust storm straight out of the *Wizard of Oz* movie-set ran amok a quarter mile to our south. Through wind-induced tears, I laughed again and yelled "GIVE ME MORE!"

We put our heads down and finally arrived in Del Norte at 7PM, where we first hit the convenience store to guzzle some chocolate milk (a great carbo re-load source) and then invaded a local brewery for pizza and a beer. We settled in for the night at a dump called the Country Family Inn, which was neither country, nor suitable for families.

Despite the washboard and the late-day winds, Day 23 was a great day on the Tour Divide. We covered the 113 miles that we planned that morning, suffered no hardships or setbacks, and did not expend massive energy. Tour-induced amnesia was doing its job as I had already forgotten about the unpleasant two days in the wind that preceded this one.

From Del Norte, we had about 770 miles to go to Antelope Wells. We knew that the next two days had massive climbs (over 15,000 cumulative feet) which would likely reduce our daily mileage, including a 4,000+-foot climb first thing the next morning to Indiana Pass at close to 12,000 feet. I still aspired to average 100 miles a day for a 30-day finish, but was quite cognizant of the gaping chasm on Tour that separates hope from reality.

Gorgeous morning for a ride into them thar hills

Chuck loves his snacks!

Winding up to Carnero Pass

Desert above Del Norte

Chapter 35 - "I remember the first time I drove through Indiana watching semis hauling grain to the west, they're gonna make it all the way to Colorado where the mountains touch the sky and rivers bend"
— The Samples, *Indiana*

Tour Divide Day 24 - 83 Miles from Del Norte, CO to campsite just short of New Mexico border. Day 24 finally gave us a good old-fashioned bike-riding no-wind-no-mud-no-washboard-no-heat-no-issue day on the Tour Divide. The day began with yet another beautiful crisp sunny Colorado morning. It was the 13th or 14th straight morning without rain. After fleeing from our flea-trap motel, we grabbed provisions at the nearest convenience store and had wheels rolling at 7:15AM. The day started with a mellow 11-miles on country pavement that climbed 800 feet from town.

At the 11-mile mark, the pavement turned to gravel and dirt and the incline lifted sharply from a three percent grade to a nine percent to ten percent grade that continued relentlessly for seven miles and 2,200 feet of elevation. I chose a reggae playlist for this climb. Three miles into the ascent, I saw my fifth bear of the Tour. He was a gargantuan black bear who crossed the trail 200 yards in front of me. I tried to take a picture, but he moved off immediately when he saw me . . . or smelled me. Or maybe he simply did not like Bob Marley!

At mile 19 of the day, my odometer hit 2,000 miles. I stared uncomprehendingly at the computer screen. 2,000 miles. I had ridden a distance equivalent to Washington D.C. to Boston, then over to Detroit, then down to Cincinnati, and then back to Washington D.C.. I'm sorry, but that is nuts.

We crested Indiana Pass at mile 22 at 11AM. At 11,960 feet, Indiana Pass was the highest point on the Tour Divide. The next 19 miles meandered in and out and up and down a network of ATV roads behind Indiana Pass, mostly staying above 11,000 feet. We rode by dazzling rock formations, a massive mining operation, several picturesque log cabins, and a splendiferous mountain lake, all while adding another 3,000 feet of cumulative elevation gain from the ups and downs. As these were ATV trails, lawless marauders often passed us in their four-wheeled buggies. Okay, they were probably nice people, but the dust kicked up from their rear wheels made them ruffians in my book.

At mile 44, we finally started descending after a morning filled with over 7,000 feet of elevation gain. A few miles into the descent, we arrived at the village of Platoro (actually more of an "outpost" than a village) and stopped at the Sky Line Lodge for an annoyingly overpriced lunch. As we entered the dining area, we were surprised to see Mario and Vincent sitting at a table. We checked the Tour Divide Trackleaders website when we left Del Norte and saw that they spent the night a few miles from Indiana Pass. Their presence at the Lodge did not compute, as they should have been 30 or 40 miles ahead of us. Seeing the inquisitive look on my face as I entered the dining room, Vincent quickly shared, "My derailleur snapped on one of the descents above Platoro and there is no fix."

I asked, "Why not just take the derailleur off and convert the bike to a single-speed?"

Vincent responded, "We considered that, but we don't think we can get the chain to fit securely on any one rear cog and we are some 300 miles from the nearest bike-shop. We have already ordered a replacement, but what sucks is that Platoro only receives mail delivery on Tuesdays and Fridays. Sooooo, it looks like we are stuck here for a couple days until Tuesday delivery."

"Jeez," I retorted, "that sucks guys. But it's good to see you both again."

I felt badly, but we could not do anything for them.

After spending lunch exchanging trail stories from the last week, we replenished our food and water at the Lodge's lobby store, and said our final goodbyes to Mario and Vincent. Sadly, we would not see them again.

From Platoro, we had a wondrous 18-mile descent that paralleled a river that bisected a lush mountain valley filled with horse farms, communes and scenic meadows, and ended in the village of Horca, CO at 7PM. This valley was the land that time forgot as there was no cell service, Wi-Fi or, in several spots, electricity.

After a quick snack in Horca, we jumped back on our bikes and climbed five miles on pavement to La Manga Pass, followed by a goose-bump generating five-mile descent as the night air turned cold.

At mile 83, we intersected with my college buddy John ("Wobber") Wontrobski. Wobber rode his motorcycle eight hours from Telluride to say hello and surprise us with a grocery bag filled with an assortment of delectable snacks and beverages. Ancient Navajo tribe elders ascribe the term "Tour Angels" to those who provide surprise help or provisions on the Tour Divide route. Or maybe it is just Tour Divide veterans who say that. I had ridden my bike for 24 straight days and was clearly making shit up. Regardless of who said it, we technically were not supposed to accept anything from Wobber because I knew him beforehand. Screw technically. None of us was winning the race and he WAS a frickin' angel in our books (not to mention great friend)! Rule violation #7?

We were hoping to cover more than 83 miles. However, Wobber found us at 10PM, and the ensuing few miles contained a steep and rocky climb into New Mexico. Already having climbed over 8,000 feet on the day, we decided to call it and set up camp for the night. We also wasted no time diving headfirst into Wobber's grocery bag of goodies.

We went to sleep with great excitement and anticipation as the next morning would take us into the final state of the Tour Divide. We had 685 miles to go.

Indiana Pass

Descending from Indiana Pass

Pristine mountain lake

Descending from Indiana Pass

Horses like singletrack too!

Chapter 36 - "And you can fly high as a kite if you want to
Faster than light if you want to
Speeding through the universe
Thinking is the best way to travel"
— The Moody Blues, *Best Way to Travel*

Several chapters ago, I mentioned how I used music to deal with boredom or to provide inspiration or energy for certain sections of the ride. However, even without music, the ride was not as boring as an outside observer might think. For one, most of the 2731 miles were a visual feast of breathtaking beauty and natural wonder. Even some of the most desolate sections of the route such as Wyoming's Great Basin or the 24 hours of prairie south of Breckenridge, Colorado or the final paved stretch to the Mexico border were stunning in their own ways. In fact, the only sections of the ride that I found thoroughly uninteresting were the 30-mile stretch south of Wamsutter, Wyoming, the alternate section between Abiquiu, New Mexico and Cuba, New Mexico and the 50-mile stretch north of Grants, New Mexico. Really. Those were it. Even the most physically painful sections of the ride like Koko Claims, Bannack Road and the climb up to Union Pass were visually stimulating. Thus, the simple act of taking in the views or stopping to take hundreds of pictures of the views consumed multiple hours of brain time.

I filled many hours with conversation. Even when riding solo on the first day of the race, I still managed to spend an hour riding and talking with each Grace Ragland, Gary Johnson and Jacki K. Once I hooked up with Wayne, Mario and Vincent (and then Chuck), there were many discussions among us while riding and during snack breaks and meals about the route, life, family, careers, music, sports, jokes, food, gear, weather, etc. These conversations formed the basis for potential lifelong friendships, particularly with Wayne, as he is the one with whom I spent the most time from beginning to end and with whom I had the most in common.

I have read many accounts from Tour Divide riders explaining how they used the distance, time and separation to find themselves on the Divide (or find something that was missing in their lives). Some have epiphanies about truly important things that they take for granted, such as wife, kids, friends or even career. Others have religious awakenings, as they believe that their adventure through "God's Country" has brought them closer to God or increased their spirituality.

I spent a lot of time over the long hours thinking about Lisa and my daughters and whether there are actions or deeds I might implement after the Tour to make me a better husband and/or father. I think those thoughts are common among people who leave their families for extended periods while their "hearts grow fonder" from absence. As for discovering the meaning of life or experiencing a religious awakening, neither of those things happened. At 50 years old, I arrived in Banff secure in my spiritual beliefs (or, more appropriately, non-beliefs) and satisfied with my place and direction in life. As shared throughout this narrative, my purpose in racing the Tour Divide was to seek adventure, challenge myself and, most importantly, raise money and awareness for First Descents. I was easily achieving those three goals and thus my thoughts during the course of the journey remained earthbound (as opposed to spiritual or metaphysical).

By far the biggest brain drain on the Tour Divide was logistics. For 30 days, my cerebrum revved in overdrive calculating miles, calculating fluid intake, calculating calories, calculating finances, calculating coming elevation gains and estimated ride times and weather contingencies and clothing choices and lodging options and pain-management and gear malfunctions and road/trail conditions and resupply points and electronics power management. There was stress associated with all of this "thinking" and it was not until a good two to three weeks after the Tour that I realized the extent of that stress and why so many Tour veterans say that the mental exhaustion they feel following the Tour Divide is every bit as debilitating as the physical exhaustion. While there were definitely many occasions where I "zoned out" on the ride, a day on the Divide surprisingly required far more brain functioning than a typical day in the life.

Chapter 37 - "I hear a voice calling, calling out for me
These shackles I've made in an attempt to be free
Be it for reason, be it for love
I won't take the easy road"
— First Aid Kit, *My Silver Lining*

Tour Divide Day 25 - 110 miles - Campsite just north of New Mexico border to Abiquiu, New Mexico. Our last night in Colorado was a chilly one, so we were up early to shake the bones. For breakfast, we helped ourselves to the last of Trail Angel Wobber's provisions, said our goodbyes and heartfelt thanks to Wobber, and then hit the trail south. We had a brief descent from the campsite followed by a rock-strewn three-mile climb that topped out at the New Mexico border with entry into the Carson National Forest.

I stared at the New Mexico entry sign in disbelief and then looked at Wayne and Chuck and said, "Holy crap, I can't believe we made it to New Mexico!"

Wayne responded, "Frickin' awesome, buddy."

Chuck responded, "Great job, men!"

After the provinces of Alberta and British Columbia, and the states of Montana, Idaho, Wyoming, Colorado, Confusion, Panic and Elation, we now entered our last state of the Tour Divide. Jubilation quickly succumbed to the realization that we still had 685 hardscrabble miles to go.

From the border, we spent the next several hours on an old narrow Jeep trail climbing and descending, climbing and descending, climbing and climbing and climbing and sweating and finally swearing thanks to a steep rocky incline that required 20 minutes of hike-a-bike to the top of an overlook called Brazo's Ridge. Like The Wall, Fleecer Ridge and the Great Basin, Brazos Ridge takes its place in Tour Lore because of the amazing views and because of the challenges associated with the trails that lead up to and away from the Ridge. During rainy years, this section of trail is supposedly impassable with thick pasty concrete New Mexican mud that rivals Bannack Road in Montana. Having already sacrificed our souls to the Gods of Mud, Filth and Muck, we were thankfully granted dry passage through Brazo's Ridge and permission to indulge happily in the expansive views of multiple mountain ridges.

The trails over the first 40 miles in New Mexico were quite rocky, rutted and rooty, and overall more technical than anything we experienced in Colorado or Wyoming. I loved it. However, my roadie brethren Wayne and Chuck struggled with this terrain and began to tire, slow down and dehydrate. To make matters worse (but comical), Wayne got bounced around so much that his 'stuff' kept flying off his bike. First, it was his maps. Then it was a jacket strapped to a back bag. Then his water bottle. At one point, Chuck and I waited a good ten minutes for Wayne to catch up. Just as we were about to backtrack to make sure Wayne was okay, he suddenly materialized with a shit-eating grin and claimed, "Oh my gawd, I was getting totally tossed by the rocks up there when suddenly my bike bags opened up and ALL of my stuff went flying in ALL directions! Total comedy. It was a yard-sale without a crash."

If only we could have gotten that on video!

At mile 47, we joined up with two other riders, one of whom was Ron J from Butts Cabin, and began a five-mile climb on a road that supposedly ended at a campground that offered a water pump. I still felt fresh and crushed the climb, arriving at the top almost a half-hour before Wayne, Chuck and the other two guys. During that half-hour, I rode over to the campground and found the entrance gate closed and locked. I bypassed the gate and attempted to use the water pump. No dice. Out of service. There was a lake a half-mile down the road, but off the route. This was decision time for me. Wayne and Chuck would certainly opt to divert to the lake for water as they were running low. I calculated that I had enough fluids to continue without wasting a likely 45-60 minutes visiting the lake.

When Wayne and Chuck arrived, I laid out the situation — "Guys, we still have 58 miles to Abiquiu and it is almost 4pm. There is no water at the campground, but there is a lake a half-mile down the road. There are a couple towns between here and Abiquiu, but I don't know if there are any stores or supplies. I have enough fluids to get to Abiquiu, but we have to hustle if we are going to make it there by a reasonable hour. What are you guys thinking?"

Wayne did not hesitate, saying, "Brent, I am thirsty, hot and fried. I need water pronto and then I only want to ride another 20 miles or so, get to bed early and start at 4Am tomorrow."

I looked at Chuck and he said, "I need water too and I don't have the legs to go the next 58 miles at your pace."

Wayne's plan was a non-starter for me. I was not sleeping well at night and did not find a pre-4AM wake-up appealing. I told Wayne and Chuck that I was going to pedal on, try to complete the 110 miles to Abiquiu by 10PM, get a full night of rest, and wait for them in the morning.

Wayne said, "May the force be with you, Luke."

Chuck said, "I don't want to hold you back, so I'll stick with Wayne."

I left them at 4PM.

It felt strange to take off solo. Throughout the journey, I often rode ahead a few miles or lagged behind a few miles, but had not truly ridden solo since days 1 and 2 of the Tour. Besides, nobody was truly solo those first days as all 182 racers were still bunched together. At this point in the race, everyone was widely spread out. Excluding Wayne, Chuck and the other two guys, the next closest racer was at least 60 miles ahead of us. By the time Wayne and Chuck got water and resumed riding, they would be some 15 miles behind me. Additionally, the next 25 to 40 miles of the route continued through a section of the Carson National Forest that technically was closed to the public that day because of forest fires. In fact, forest fires and dangerously dry conditions forced the closure of most of the parks and forests in New Mexico. We later learned that "authorities" would have blocked our entrance to Carson National Forest and rerouted us with a pavement detour if we had arrived over the weekend. However, since we arrived at Carson early on a Monday morning, the authorities must have gone home after the weekend. Thus, I was literally the only human on the trail for the next 40 miles. It was liberating, as I could go my own speed without stopping or waiting, but also kind of freaky.

At the 75-mile mark, I passed through the village of Vallecitos. Vallecitos would otherwise earn no mention on the Tour Divide but for a collection of mangy stray dogs that inhabit the village and that make sport of chasing bikers up the only street in town. To heighten the challenge for the dogs' prey (their "prey" being me!), the only street through town goes uphill over a quarter-mile stretch. I pedaled speedily and stealthily through the village with my bear spray unlocked and my eyes manically darting back and forth. To my relief and amusement, only one canine mongrel chased me, and he was a pathetic three-legged snarling Spuds Mackenzie-resembling mutt that I was easily able to outpace.

After the last ramshackle house in Vallecitos, the road immediately re-entered the Carson Nat'l Forest and continued for another 16 miles with one long climb and one long descent before arriving in the town of El Rito. By then it was 8PM and I was famished. I had not seen a store or restaurant since Platoro 130 miles ago and was down to my last Clif Bar. Wobber's arrival with food the evening before was becoming more trail angelic by the minute. To my chagrin, nothing was open in El Rito. This left me no choice but to hurriedly press on to Abiquiu. Fortunately, I had cell service in El Rito, so I called Lisa and asked her to try to find me a bed in Abiquiu while I started the last 18 miles.

About a half hour out of El Rito and after a wonderful ten mile downhill on pavement, I called Lisa for a lodging update. She relayed that all hotel rooms in town were booked, but there was a guesthouse with availability one and a half miles past town. I said, "Sounds great! Please book it."

I arrived in Abiquiu at 9PM ready to feast at the first open store or restaurant. Damn! NOTHING was open and I had long since consumed and digested my last Clif bar. With no other options, I rode to the guesthouse (called 'Las Parras de Abiquiu') and was met at the door by the owners, Erin and Stan. Taking immediate pity on my bedraggled countenance, Erin plied me with an assortment of fruit, a salami sandwich, two candy bars, a Dr Pepper, nuts, raisins and potato chips. Bonus of all bonuses, adjacent to my room was a washer/dryer. I took less than 15 minutes to voraciously scarf down everything listed above, shower, and throw every odious piece of clothing I possessed into the washing machine. I then spent the next two hours blissfully lounging in a soft terry-cloth robe, catching up on emails and Facebook, and crafting my daily blog on my iPhone. I also sent a text message to Wayne's wife Jan to let her know why my dot displayed on Trackleaders.com was so far ahead of Wayne's dot and to assure her that everything was okay.

Before going to sleep for the night, I walked in front of a full-length mirror in the bathroom and was dumbfounded to see my reflection. I was nothing but sinews, skin and bones. Although there was no scale in the room, I was pretty sure that I was down to my sophomore year weight . . . from high school!!

There were 577 miles to go. I was starting to taste it!

Thanks Trail Angel Wobber!

Climb to Brazo's Ridge

Descent to El Rito

El Rito National Monument

Clean!!

Chapter 38 - "Twenty twenty twenty four hours to go
I wanna be sedated
Nothing to do, nowhere to go-o-o,
I wanna be sedated"
— The Ramones, *I Wanna Be Sedated*

Tour Divide Day 26 - 104 miles from Abiquiu, NM to a field southwest of Cuba, NM. On the Tour Divide, nothing ever goes as planned, the expected usually results in the unexpected, and there is no such thing as an easy day. There are only hard days, harder days and puke. Do not get me wrong, most of the hard days are still fantastic . . . except those that suck.

I opened my eyes at 6:30AM in the glorious comfort of the Las Parras de Abiquiu and immediately logged onto the Trackleaders website to check Wayne and Chuck's progress. It appeared that they made good on the 4AM start and would arrive in Abiquiu at around 8:15AM. Ratfarts! I was hoping they would arrive later so I could chill longer in my plush bed. While brushing my teeth, I noticed a bowl of Epsom salts next to the bathtub. Hmmm, a hot Epsom salt bath sounded like a delicious way to start a well-balanced day. And it soooooo was. After the bath, I packed my stuff, lathered myself with sunscreen and A & D Ointment (a taint's only real friend), happily adorned myself with my clean and wonderfully non-malodorous clothes, paid my bill, and pedaled over to the convenience store to meet Wayne and Chuck.

Before heading into the store, I performed an elaborate sacrificial ceremony and dispensed with my trusty can of bear-spray. Although I never used the spray, it provided great comfort (like Linus's blanket) and I was sad to say goodbye. Okay, that was melodramatic bullshit. I was happy to get rid of the weight.

Over a breakfast consisting of three bacon-egg-and-cheese breakfast sandwiches, two bananas and three pop-tarts, Wayne and Chuck shared their plight from the day before. After I left them, they descended to the lake to seek water and found the lake to be a duck-infested algae-covered cesspool. Even with filters and raging thirst, they were unwilling to drink the lake water. Next to the lake was a dumpster. Chuck looked at Wayne and said, "I guess we need to dive."

Wayne looked at Chuck uncomprehendingly and responded, "If we can't drink the water, why the hell would we want to dive in it?"

Chuck retorted, "Not the lake, the dumpster! We need to 'dumpster-dive!'"

With trepidation, they raised the dumpster lid, leaned into the dumpster, rummaged around, found a few unfinished water bottles, and proceeded to finish them. Wayne said, "That was by far one of my scariest moments on the Tour as I was thoroughly unable to focus or think straight because of dehydration. Jeez, I actually drank from a dumpster bottle!"

With my own stomach doing somersaults after hearing their story, I decided not to talk about my fabulous night in the guesthouse!

From Abiquiu, the Tour Divide route headed due south into the Santa Fe National Forest, up into the mountains above Abiquiu, and across a giant mesa before dropping into the town of Cuba. However, with the outbreak of forest fires throughout New Mexico, the Santa Fe Forest was closed and we were re-routed via paved roads to Cuba. I hated to deviate from the route. I was also upset to miss the views from the mesa. However, we had no choice. At least the paved roads would provide an easy ride and big mileage.

Easy ride. That is funny. And where, boys and girls, do false expectations typically lead? That is right, disappointment. I despise false expectations.

Other than a great view of Lake Abiquiu during the first few miles, the paved route was a boring suckfest. Worst of all, our old arch-nemesis, Sir Stifford Headwind, Duke of Suckington, turned an anticipated relaxing five-hour jaunt into an aggravating eight-hour grind. The only positive of the entire eight hours was a stop at a diner halfway to Cuba that served the best ice cream that side of . . . Abiquiu.

We arrived in Cuba at 5PM and immediately stocked up on food and fluids as our next section was 124 miles from Cuba, New Mexico to the town of Grants, New Mexico and the maps were unclear whether there were open stores on the route. Then we hit McDonald's because (a) it was the first one we had seen since Fernie on Day 3, and (b) because Chuck was epileptically craving it. After a Big Mac, six McNuggets, large fries, chocolate milkshake and two chocolate-chip cookies (and similar meals for both Chuck and Wayne), none of us felt motivated to return to our bikes. Moreover, the temperature was still in the low 90s and the wind was still blowing hard in the wrong direction. Wayne was close to throwing in the towel and getting a room in Cuba. I could not blame him as he had been riding since 4AM. I had to somehow wean him off this 4AM option that he relished.

Our goal was to get to Grants by the following evening. Wayne's 4AM option required us to ride the entire 124 miles in one day. I hated that plan. I feared that 124 miles would be impossibly torturous if we had another full day of headwinds. I suggested that we ride from the McDonalds and try to get in 20-25 miles, as "only" 99-104 miles the next day would be much more feasible. This pondering and discussing and ruminating and procrastinating and pontificating and negotiating went on for over an hour until we finally decided at 7:15 to start riding. This is where the expected turned into the unexpected . . . and finally in a good way. We expected a shitty ride into the evening. Instead, within 15 minutes of leaving Mickey D's, the temperature cooled into the high 70s and the wind stopped as if someone had the pulled the plug on the giant sky fan.

We rode for two hours and knocked out 27 miles, leaving us with 97 for the next day.

Digression alert! In Ocean City, Maryland, there is a bar/restaurant called Fager's Island that faces west over the Assawoman Bay. No snickering. That is actually the name of the bay. Anyway, every night during the summer, Tchaikovsky's 1812 Overture plays at sunset with the song timed perfectly to reach its cannon-blaring crescendo just as the last slivers of sunlight disappear over the bay. As the sun set over the mountains south of Grants and we reached the base of a climb, I drew inspiration from Fager's and blasted the 1812 Overture on my Bluetooth speaker. When the initial symphony notes sounded, Wayne and Chuck both gave me "what the fuck?" looks. I implored them to just stop talking, pedal, and listen.

We pedaled in silence to the sound and flow of the music, and crested the climb just as the final cannons blasted, the Russian army defeated Napoleon, and the last orange rays of the sun disappeared over the horizon. It was a magical, surreal, and transcendent moment that the three of us will never forget.

We continued another half-hour led by the narrow beams of our headlights before coming upon a convenience store that was about to close for the night. We indulged in ice cream, popsicles and chocolate milk, and learned from the counter clerk that the store re-opened at 6AM with an assortment of breakfast foods. The clerk also welcomed us to sleep in a little dirt courtyard behind the store. Upon inspection, excessive light bathed the courtyard and broken glass coated the dirt surface.

We got back on our bikes and rode a few hundred yards past the store, finding an area of flat ground tucked behind shrubs along the side of the road. As it was a warm evening with a clear sky, we did not bother pitching our tents. We just laid our pads and sleeping bags on the ground and slept under the stars, serenaded by the sounds of coyotes and crickets. The peaceful perfection of my starlit slumber was only diminished by my inflatable sleeping pad's springing a leak and refusing to stay inflated. No matter. There were only three or four nights left of our Tour and I was barely sleeping anyway. I would deal with it. I had no choice. There were 473 miles to go.

Goodbye bear spray. It's been real.

Lake Abiquiu - the only pretty view of the whole day

Sunset to 1812 Overture

Sleeping without cover

Chapter 39 - "Gray skies are gonna clear up, Put on a happy face
Brush off the clouds and cheer up, Put on a happy face
And if you're feeling cross and bitterish
Don't sit and whine;
Think of banana splits and licorice
And you'll feel fine"
— Dick Van Dyke, *Bye Bye Birdie - Put on a Happy Face*

Tour Divide - Day 27 - 95 miles from Field south of Cuba, NM to Grants, NM. After a restless night of sleep due to my deflated sleeping pad, the morning started cheerily with sunny skies, a distant rooster crowing, a whiff of light breeze, breakfast and resupply at the convenience store. Our initial pace was relaxed and we stopped after two hours at the Chaco Laundromat/Convenience store at mile 21. Humorously, none of us needed anything in Chaco. However, a convenience store on the Tour Divide is like a gift shop at the airport. How so? Well, how many times have you carried two packs of gum, a sandwich from Subway, a full bottle of water, two newspapers, three magazines and an e-book on your tablet and still felt compelled to stop in the airport gift shop to buy additional magazines and snacks? Truth be told, what caught my eye was a sign in front of the Chaco store offering Grape Shasta. I had not seen Grape Shasta since I was a kid at Bar-T-Ranch day camp in Maryland. The mere words triggered an instant craving and I had to have some of that bubbly purple goodness. So my first food stop of the day consisted of a creamsicle (don't ask), a can of grape Shasta and . . . an apple because, ya know, I was trying to eat healthily and it WAS only 8:30 in the morning.

The next 20 miles after Chaco passed quickly, but infernal heat set in (97.7 degrees on my Garmin), so at 11:30AM we found the only tree in the desert and plopped down in the shade for a snack break. I ate a turkey sandwich and then reclined on my back and took a 20-minute nap. This was my first and only mid-day nap on the entire Tour. Meanwhile, the terrain was surprisingly uninteresting, unless you like smoldering pavement, and the views were vapid and yawn inspiring . . . just endless miles of flat brown rocky desert. In fact, the best way to describe the land along this route is to think of the opening scene in Episode One of *Breaking Bad* when Walter White cooked crystal meth in a camper in the desert outside of Albuquerque. We were not too far from Albuquerque, so maybe this was the place!

At mile 50, the light wind slightly kicked up and pirouetted into our faces. This unsettled us. For seven days in a row, the afternoon breezes had turned into savage headwinds from the south. To say we were tired of the wind is like saying that we were TIRED OF THE FUCKING WIND!! Sorry, I was metaphorically challenged by Day 27. Or was that a simile? Whatever. In addition to the wind, I had been struggling for days with multiple stinging saddle sores that made it difficult to sit in any one position for more than 30 seconds at a time. To alleviate the contact sting, I constantly slid my butt forwards, backwards, left and right. This issue would stick with me through the rest of the Tour, not getting any better, but fortunately not getting much worse.

    I needed something to take my mind off the saddle sores and the impending misery that the changing wind was about to rain down on us (though actual rain would have been nice at that moment). Sorta kinda summoning Michael Keaton in *Beetlejuice,* I decided that "It's showtime!" I reached into my quiver of music playlists and pulled out the Showtunes playlist that I had been saving for the just the right occasion. I hit shuffle and then play. First up was a medley from *Grease,* followed by songs from *Hamilton, Pippin, LaLaLand, Mary Poppins, Greatest Showman, Wicked, Phantom of the Opera, Les Miserab*les and *Joseph and the Amazing Technicolor Dreamcoat.* By the time the dulcet voice of Julie Andrews warbled the dynamic duo of *Edelweiss* and *The Lonely Goatherd* from the *Sound of Music* at mile 60, the wind was ferociously howling in our faces. Even *Chim-Chiminy-Chim-Chiminy-Chim-Chim-Chiree* could not cure the foul mood rapidly overtaking the boys and me. *The Phaaaaaaaaantom of the Opera* is (clearly) here . . . inside my mind!

    At mile 74, we started an apparent 20-mile descent into the town of Grants. I say "apparent" because it looked downhill and because the gradient on my bike computer showed a negative three percent gradient. However, even on downhill pavement, we worked our asses off just to exceed ten miles per hour. If we stopped pedaling for five seconds, the wind brought us to a complete stop . . . going downhill! Screw you *Hakuna Matata* and *Bippety Boppety Boo*! You are not helping!

    With ten miles to go before Grants, the wind whipped so hard that if we were at the beach, mass-murder by impaling would be committed against unsuspecting sun-worshippers by an army of heavy umbrellas blowing across the sand. Our misery index had eclipsed Defcon 5! (I am not a tech or science-fiction guy, so I assume Defcon 5 is pretty bad.) We needed food, we needed rest and we needed shelter from the wind.

    On the outskirts of Grants, we turned onto the famous Route 66, which would take us right through the center of town. Back in the early 20th century, Route 66 was the major highway that connected the Midwest to the California coast, and Route 66 towns like Grants flourished. With the construction of major interstates in the 1950s and 1960s, the economies and populations of towns like Grants declined as through-traffic disappeared overnight.

Riding into town, we witnessed the remnants of a once-thriving community now overrun by vacancy signs, dilapidated buildings, rusted fences, and potholed parking lots. Fortunately, rising like a Phoenix from the ashes of Grants towered a shining beacon of American ingenuity — the ubiquitous and beautiful McDonalds' golden arches. Without warning, our bikes abruptly swerved across the highway in front of moving traffic, dashed into the McDonalds' parking lot, and skidded to a squealing stop in front of the entrance. Sorry officer, it was not me, it was my angry bike. And it was not really a skidding stop. It was more of a slow amble followed by a resigned dismount.

The plan was to drown our fatigue in milkshakes, load the digestive system with thousands of empty calories and then head out and try to ride 20 to 25 more miles, similar to the previous evening. I inhaled two double quarter-pounders with cheese, a large fries, a chocolate milkshake, a blue icy swirlie thing, two snickerdoodle cookies and nine cups of ice water. While my appetite for sustenance was sated, my appetite to resume rotating my feet around my front chain-ring several thousand more times that day was gone with the wind (no pun intended as I did not have any *Gone With the Wind* songs on my playlist). We stared ruefully out the window at the stiffly blowing American flags on every street lamp (it being July 4th) and then said to hell with more riding and called the nearby Motel 6 to reserve rooms. I owed Wayne participation in at least one early-to-bed-early-to-rise plan of attack before the Tour reached its conclusion!

I was tired of the wind. I was tired of bitching about the wind. For non-bikers, I hope this narrative adequately conveys how demoralizing it was/is to wage war with a persistent blustery headwind, particularly with fat tires and 55-60 pounds of bike plus gear. Winds were certainly not rare in that part of the country. However, eight straight days of tree-bending wind from the same direction (south to north) was abnormal. This particularly sucked considering our riding direction was north to south. By the way, please do not mistake my whining with a lack of perspective. I fully recognized at the time and as I type this tale that suffering through a windy bike ride in boring terrain was anything but a hardship in the greater scheme. But damn if it did not squeeze the enjoyment out of some of those final days of the Tour.

After checking into the Motel 6 (where nobody left the lights on for us

– damn you Tom Bodett!), we walked over to the neighboring Walgreens to purchase food for the next day. Coincidentally, there were four other Tour Divide riders also wandering the Walgreens' aisles, and accidentally smacking into things like shelves and display stands and Walgreen's employees and fellow customers. Walgreens may as well have been the movie set for the next zombie apocalypse film as we all aimlessly stumbled back and forth with identical 1,000-yard blank stares.

On the bright side, despite the fatigue, heat, wind and ennui, we still managed to cover 95 miles on Day 27, thus leaving us with only 375 miles to the finish. The next day would be one of the most important days of the Tour, as it would dictate whether we would make the 30-day finish. I was too tired that evening to review maps and calculate options, so the plan was to awaken at 3:45AM, meet for breakfast at Denny's across the street, and give it a 'good old college try' to loosely plan the next three days.

My dorm room last night

Breakfast

Chillin' in the Chaco laundromat

Nap tree

Searching for Walter White

Chapter 40 – "Well, I won't back down,
No I won't back down
You can stand me up at the gates of hell
But I won't back down"
— Tom Petty, *I Won't Back Down*

In Chapter 37, I posited that I experienced no life-changing epiphanies or spiritual awakenings on the Tour Divide. Regardless, my Tour was chockfull of deep soulful reflections, particularly during poignant visual moments like cresting Priest Pass in Montana in the gloaming, traversing the Wind River Valley in Wyoming, or the symphonic ride into the sunset after Cuba, New Mexico. A particularly vivid section of introspection occurred on my solo ride through the publicly closed Carson National Forest *en route* to Abiquiu, New Mexico. With knowledge that no rescue services were available if I suffered a mishap, I thought conceptually about risk, reward, and regret.

To an outsider, the Tour Divide was not just a crazy adventure, but a crazy risk. Innumerable things could go wrong, many of which could put life and limb in jeopardy. Why would I want to expose myself knowingly to such peril? How and where does one draw the line between risk and reward, between smart and stupid, and/or between safe and reckless?

Oxymoronically, I consider myself a conservative risk-taker. I like pushing the envelope, whether recreationally, professionally or financially, but believe that most of the risks I have taken in life are educated, and most (but not all) will not result in bodily harm . . . or a casket. I am not burdened by many fears, except one. I fear regret.

Through my work and affiliation with First Descents, I have spoken to and spent time with dozens and dozens of cancer fighters and survivors of all ages. The common yearning among survivors, aside from the simple will to live, is to live without regret. These brave individuals have taught (and shown) me that life is finite and short and our time could end instantaneously. They espouse taking chances, taking risks, following dreams, never saying "I can't," accomplishing tasks today instead of tomorrow, saying "I love you" often and loud, disregarding fear, worry and trepidation as useless unproductive emotions, and, most of all, living without regret. These conversations are my life-fuel.

Additionally, I draw inspiration from the arts, often appropriating and animating quotes and pithy catch phrases. One such phrase is from the movie 'Dead Poets Society' when Robin Williams' character gives a speech to his students that ends with, "Carpe diem, seize the day boys, make your lives extraordinary." I swear allegiance to *carpe diem*. Another is the final sentence from the Robert Frost poem *The Road Not Taken* that says, "Two roads diverged in the wood and I, I took the one less travelled by, and that has made all the difference."

For me, seeking challenges, leaping out of the box of comfort, following an oft-lonely path, and taking occasional risks are as necessary for regret-prevention as oxygen is for breathing. While risks sometimes result in their own regrets, the old adage applies — what doesn't kill you makes you stronger. Mistakes and failures are inevitable and are equally as necessary for growth as successes and rewards. Additionally, mistakes and failures often become fodder for great stories (such as some of the stories within this book)!

One of my favorite historical passages is Teddy Roosevelt's "Man in the Arena" from the "Citizenship in a Republic" speech he delivered 1923. The passage requires no synopsis as its meaning is clear and concise. I believe Roosevelt's words apply directly to those of us who voluntarily take on challenges like the Tour Divide. Movies, books and newspaper editorials have quoted the speech *ad nauseam,* but what the hell, here it is again:

> *"It is not the critic who counts; not the man who points out how the strong man stumbles, or where the doer of deeds could have done them better. The credit belongs to the man who is actually in the arena, whose face is marred by dust and sweat and blood; who strives valiantly; who errs, who comes short again and again, because there is no effort without error and shortcoming; but who does actually strive to do the deeds; who knows great enthusiasms, the great devotions; who spends himself in a worthy cause; who at the best knows in the end the triumph of high achievement, and who at the worst, if he fails, at least fails while daring greatly, so that his place shall never be with those cold and timid souls who neither know victory nor defeat."*

Chapter 41 – "And all the years will come and go,
   take us up, always up.
   We may never pass this way again.
   We may never pass this way again.
   We may never pass this way again.
   Dreams, so they say, are for the fools
   and they let 'em drift away."
   — Seals and Crofts, *We May Never Pass This Way Again*

Tour Divide Day 28 - 131 Miles from Grants, NM to somewhere in the Gila WIlderness, NM. The laborious ride to Grants and the post-ride meltdown in McDonald's left my psyche in tatters. I went to sleep at the Motel 6 resolved to put all negativity behind me and start fresh from Denny's. Throughout this story, I have alluded to the goal of finishing in less than 30 days. However, we never let the 30-day goal drive us or influence any daily riding decisions. With three days to go, 30 days was in reach and, for the first time since leaving Banff, we needed to formulate a multi-day plan.

It was Thursday morning, July 5. To accomplish a sub-30 day finish, we needed to reach the US border at Antelope Wells, NM by 7:59:59AM on Sunday morning, July 8. Anything was possible.

The alarm buzzed at 3:45AM and we formally started the morning at 4:30AM with a gourmet breakfast at Denny's. After poring over the maps, I presented an aggressive three-day plan to Wayne and Chuck. Part one of the plan required an attitude adjustment from the day before. We quickly achieved this task thanks to Denny's delectable Double-Grand Slam breakfast. Part two involved somehow someway riding 248 miles in two days and ending up in Silver City, New Mexico by the next night. From Silver City, it was an easy 125 miles to the border. Wait, bad choice of words. It *appeared* to be an easy 125 miles to the border . . . which sounds crazy when said aloud. Was there really such a thing as an "easy" 125 miles of mountain biking? I guess everything is relative.

While discussing the plan, Chuck informed us that his wife could not reach Antelope Wells until Sunday afternoon. Chuck had not followed the full Tour Divide route and was technically not participating in the race. I thus sensed hesitance on his part to push hard for a couple reasons. One, it was important for Chuck to have his wife greet him at the finish. Two, a sub 30-day finish was arbitrary and irrelevant if you were not a race participant. Adding to the plan's jeopardy, Wayne shared that his wife Jan was flying into Tucson on Sunday morning and likewise would not make it to the finish until Sunday afternoon. However, he WAS a race participant as well as a tough and competitive son-of-a-bitch. I appealed to his competitive instincts to convince him that a sub-30 day finish was more important than a spousal finish greeting. It was an easy sell!

We left Denny's at 5:30AM and immediately found a smooth rhythm and fast pace. Three miles into the ride, Chuck announced that he left his headlight at the motel and turned around to return and retrieve it. It happened so quickly that there was not even conversation. One second Chuck was with us and then he was gone. Someday I will ask him to come clean about whether he really left his light and, if so, whether he really even needed it with less than three days left, OR whether the old "left-my-light-at-the-motel" story was simply his out for not having to participate in our mad dash to the finish.

The first 38 miles from Grants were on smooth pavement that wound through the El Mapais National Conservation Area. Known as the "Badlands of the Southwest," the El Mapais National Conservation Area occupies a volcanic field and contains a series of prismatic (but dominantly orange) cliffs, canyons, arches and craters, all visible from the road.

At mile 39, we turned left onto a 32-mile stretch of dirt road that knifed through topography resembling pictures I have seen of the Saharan Steppe in Northern Africa (don't ask me to explain as I have run out of adjectives to describe "beautiful" views). Over the 32 miles, the dirt road climbed 1,000 feet through a series of short steep rises connected by flat straightaways. The road was soft in places and contained intermittent washboard, but we successfully navigated the first 70 miles in seven hours. The highlight for me occurred at mile 60. I felt great and was thrilled with our pace when we hit a groovy stretch of dirt just as a "two-fer" of Doors' songs, *Break on Through* and *LA Woman* blasted on my speaker. Striking an inner chord, I bellowed the lyrics to both songs . . . frightening a few pack mules. Maybe the moment provided deep inner meaning to breaking on through to the other side, but I could not ascribe any philosophic context poetically tying the LA Woman lyrics to my travails. Mr. MoJo was definitely risin' though! (By the way, "Mr. MoJo" is NOT an anatomical euphemism. Get your head out of the gutter and listen to the song!)

At 1PM and at almost exactly the 70-mile mark, we reached the world famous Pie Town and the Pie Town Cafe. Pie Town is known for its delicious meat loaf (just seeing if you are still paying attention; there was no meat loaf). Duh, it is known for its pies. Wayne and I split a pizza pie for lunch. Three bites of the pizza confirmed that Pie Town is not famous for its pizza pies. We then ordered real pie for dessert. I think there is a town ordinance requiring Tour Dividers to order 'real' pie or risk deportation back to Canada. I ate a chocolate custard pie and it was sublime. Wayne had the Key-Lime pie and it was apparently subLIMER. We both left positive Yelp reviews.

Chuck arrived at the Pie Town Café just as Wayne and I were loading up after a lengthy break. He did not seem concerned about falling behind and, unsurprisingly, did not ask us to wait for him. Wayne and I said farewell to Chuck, wistfully aware that we likely would not see him again. It was 2:30PM and our goal was to throw down another 60 miles before 10PM. Dark clouds were rapidly building south of us and the radar map showed multi-colored storm cells all over southern New Mexico. Our goal would be challenging.

The first ten miles out of Pie Town pointed us directly south toward the Gila Wilderness and a mass of menacing black clouds. Our immediate destiny apparently involved a nasty storm chewing us up and spitting us out. Fortuitously, the road turned due west for several miles and we successfully skirted the storm, escaping with just a few scattered drops.

At mile 94, we commenced our last monumental challenge in Tour Lore — the Gila (pronounced "Hee-La") Wilderness — otherwise known as the "Gila Monster" or simply "The Gila." Tour Divide veterans speak of The Gila with hushed reverence . . . like a scary ogre in a children's fairy tale. The Gila comprises some 560,000 acres and was once the home to Geronimo and the Apache Indians. There are no services in The Gila, which required packing enough food and water in Pie Town to carry us 184 miles. We filled every square centimeter in our various packs to the point of bursting zippers.

Typically, The Gila is deathly hot and many racers choose to ride through the night to avoid the heat. We were lucky as we arrived in The Gila mere days into the monsoon season that annually sweeps southern New Mexico in early July. While measurable rain had yet to fall, the temperatures had dropped from daily highs near 102 the prior week to the mid-80s during the last few days. This was finally some good weather luck for us. Ironically, we could attribute (and thank) the lower temperatures to the recent scourge of dastardly south winds.

Miles 94 to 110 climbed through a thick canopy forest that engulfed the dirt road. At the top of the climb, we were granted an audacious screaming descent that flattened in a huge desolate valley that was aglow (for lack of a better term) with the setting sun. The route serpentined along the base of the mountains flanking the west side of the valley. A dazzling full rainbow danced and flickered across the mountains towering over the opposite side of the valley.

The striking landscape, accentuated by the sunset, the lustrous valley, and the rainbow, was exactly what I envisioned when I created my "Going Deep – Tour Divide" playlist. I pressed 'Shuffle Play' and savored a procession of songs, each of which contained a theme or specific lyrics that uncannily and perfectly captured the moment. The title lyrics in Seals and Crofts' song *We Will Never Pass this Way Again* urged me to take in and appreciate everything around me as I would probably never do this race or witness this valley again. *My Silver Lining* by First Aid Kit contains a haunting final stanza of lyrics that say, "I won't take the easy road, easy road, easy road, no." This verse succinctly encapsulated my decision to take on this adventure. America's *Horse with No Name* could well have been a song about my bike as I was riding through a desert on a bike with no name and it felt good to be out from the rain. We were Don Henley's *Boys of Summer* and Jim Morrison's *Riders on the Storm* and Neil Young's *Dreamin' Man*. We were Kansas' wayward sons carrying on until we laid our weary heads to rest. As the sun set and the skies morphed from grey to black, we rode down the Rolling Stones' *Moonlight Mile*. Finally, as we wound on down the road, our shadows taller than our souls, there walked a lady we all knew, who shone white light and wanted to show, how everything still turns to gold, and we listened very hard, and the tune came to us at last, when we both were one and one was all, to be a rock and not to roll, and we were buying Led Zeppelin's *Stairway to Heaven*.

We quit in pitch-dark at 10PM when the odometer hit 131 miles and set up camp on a level patch of ground within a few feet of the dirt road. We had no concerns about vehicle sounds or headlights. We had not seen a single vehicle over the prior 30 miles and doubted we would see one for the next 30 miles. The Gila symbolized and epitomized the term 'remote wilderness.'

The ride from Grants to our Gila campsite officially constituted the longest ride of my life from both a mileage standpoint, beating the Wind River Wyoming ride by one mile, and from a time standpoint at over 16 hours. The next day would be grueling with significant steep elevation gains, but we felt humbly confident that our sub-30-day target would become reality as long as we avoided stupid decisions and/or bad luck.

El Mapais

El Mapais arch

Road to Pie Town

Pie Town Cafe

Entering the Gila Wilderness

Vastness of the Gila

Gila rainbow

Chapter 42 - "When you're looking for space,
           and to find out who you are
           When you're looking to try and reach the stars
           It's a sweet, sweet, sweet dream
           Sometimes I'm almost there
           Sometimes I fly like an eagle
           But sometimes I'm deep in despair
           Sometimes I fly like an eagle,
           Like an eagle, I go flying high . . ."
           — John Denver, *Looking For Space*

Tour Divide – Day 29 – 119 Miles – Gila Wilderness to Silver City, NV. Sleep came quickly last night, but continued restlessly and uncomfortably thanks to my inflatable sleeping pad that no longer inflated. Oh well. By Day 29 of the Tour, sleep was an overrated luxury. It was Friday, July 6 and it was the penultimate day (hopefully) of the Tour Divide. We awoke at 5:30AM under dawn's first rays and were moving by 6:15AM. This was going to be one of the most demanding days of the Tour, not just because of the 119 miles to Silver City, NV, but because most of the miles would cross The Gila's largest teeth, including a massive 8300+ feet of climbing on legs that were cooked from 131 miles over 16 hours the day before.

We started sluggishly (as expected) and it took three solid hours before we shook off the dull legs and found our pedal strokes. During those three hours, we continued our tour of the giant valley that so enraptured us the evening before and witnessed several wondrous animal kingdom moments including a massive herd of elk crossing the trail right in front of us, a mammoth cow bathing in a pond, a pack of mountain goats scaling a steep rocky hill, and an army of jackrabbits hopping alongside us.

After passing several private farms, we arrived at the Beaverhead Work Center at mile 39. A friendly kid working out front offered welcome and shared a little history about the facility. We were as curious as the next gals about the genesis and purpose of the facility (built to combat forest-fires in the Gila), but what really interested us was the location of their water-pump and a temperamental soda-machine glorified by Tour Lore. Fluid-replenishment was essential as we still had 80 hard miles until Silver City with no further services in between.

We cautiously approached the soda machine with fingers crossed. It appeared to be working, but we were not positive. I had visions of the mysterious Zoltar fortune-telling machine from the movie *Big*. Zoltar granted young Josh Baskin his wish to be big (turning into Tom Hanks)

239

. . . even though the machine was unplugged. Would this soda-machine grant us our wish for caffeine and sugar? Was it even plugged in? Or was this machine more like the telephone booth in *Bill and Ted's Excellent Adventure*? Would we press the Coke tab and transport to another time and place? My imagination was running amok after 29 days.

I pulled out a few one-dollar bills and reached toward the cash insert slot. With a wry grin, the friendly kid said, "Don't bother putting your money in the machine . . . unless you don't like your money!" He told us to wait a few minutes for "the guy" who had "the key." The "guy" turned out to be another friendly dude named Chris and, sure enough, he had a key to the machine (and the key to our stomachs). He opened the machine, pulled out two Cokes for me and three Cokes for Wayne and we threw him some cash.

Chris then asked, "Hey guys, are you hungry?"

Being the smart-ass that I am, I quickly responded (with a smile), "Chris, have you ever encountered a Tour Divide rider who DID NOT want something to eat?"

Chris laughed good-spiritedly, opened the door to the office, and told us to help ourselves to the contents of a box containing pastries, cookies, and chips.

Side note from Beaverhead: Chris the "Guy" was wearing a "Redskins" t-shirt. Upon closer look, I saw that it was the name of a local high school football team.

"Chris, great shirt," I said. "Just wondering if the Native-Americans at the school are offended by the name?"

Chris grinned and responded, "Amigo, the Native-Americans are more offended by the holier-than-thou politicians and celebrities feigning outrage over the Washington Redskins' team name than they are about the name itself! Hell, we actually changed the school name TO 'Redskins' several years ago just to spit in the face of the bullshit fake outrage."

Interesting.

After Beaverhead, the next 36 miles were incredible and leg crushing as well as incredibly leg crushing. We ascended and descended countless times with steep punchy climbs that each ranged in elevation gain from several hundred feet to over a thousand feet. The toil was relentless, as there were no flat run-outs between the end of a descent and the start of the next climb. These hills were the unremitting fangs of The Gila.

At mile 75, after hour upon hour traversing the roof of the Gila, we mercifully began a long relaxing descent that dropped us several thousand feet over 15 miles.

It was past 8PM by the time we reached the bottom of the descent and we still faced 26 miles (containing two significant climbs) before reaching Silver City. We were running on fumes after 14 hours of riding with thousands of feet of leg-churning climbs. The last big climb of the day was a monster consisting of 11 miles of single-track on the Continental Divide hiking trail ("CDT") starting with a half-mile of steep hike-a-bike.

The trailhead for the CDT is located behind the Sapillo Group Campground. We pulled into the campground and found a festive atmosphere brimming with RVs, colorful tents, kids, ATVs, and generally happy people excited for the weekend. Before reaching the CDT trailhead, we passed a large family of men, women and children sitting in an elongated circle. Wayne was running low on water and unabashedly approached the group to beg for water. I suppose they took great pity on us from the weary looks on our faces and the low shrugs of our shoulders as they not only topped off our waters, but also gave us peaches and oranges. Summoning the unofficial powers unofficially vested in me by the unofficial Crazy Larry, I unofficially enshrined them all in the unofficial "Trail Angels" hall of fame.

With peach juices streaming down our faces thanks to our culinary slobbery, we profusely thanked our family campers, made our way to the CDT trailhead, and stared up at a mini-wall. We looked at each other with sighs, dismounted our bikes and started hiking up. Over the first twenty-five to thirty steps, I audibly cursed the race directors for subjecting us to a steep hike-a-bike right on the heels of the Gila when there exists an alternate route that involves bicycle riding instead of hiking.

The hike continued another ten minutes before the trail leveled enough to remount our bikes. To my surprise and delight, it then morphed into a phenomenal frickin' mountain bike trail! The only problem was that it wasn't a phenomenal frickin' mountain bike trail for Wayne. In fact, for him it was just *frickin'* as the trail was off-camber, overgrown with high grass and bushes, and nastily exposed. In mountain biking, as in hiking, 'exposure' means that one false move and you may be tumbling hundreds of feet down a steep hill or over a cliff (i.e., you are 'exposed' to tumbling hundreds of feet down a steep hill or over a cliff). I have ridden trails like this for 20 years and was ecstatic. Wayne had never experienced anything like this and quickly proclaimed, "No effin' way buddy, I'm walking!"

Wayne's declaration sparked a huge dilemma. I calculated that it would take him between three and four hours to walk this trail. I could ride the whole thing in about an hour. I did not want to leave him, but man it was going to be painful to ride a few minutes and then wait, ride a few minutes and then wait, and so on. At one of my initial waits, Lisa texted me on my

Garmin to say, "It's getting late, are you okay?" I shared my predicament with regard to Wayne and she replied without hesitation that I must stay with him unless he orders me — not tells me, not suggests to me, not asks me —to go on without him.

I rode another 100 yards up the trail and stopped to wait again. I thought about Lisa's directive and decided to not say anything to Wayne and just see how things played out. After another 10 minutes of me repeatedly shooting ahead and waiting, Wayne came around a bend and said, "Brent, this is ridiculous, please get the hell out of here and I'll meet you in Silver City by morning."

In the most sympathetic voice I could summon, I asked, "Wayne, are you sure? I hate to leave you out here by yourself."

Without blinking, Wayne responded, "I am a big boy and not only would it be absurd for you to spend three to four hours out here waiting for me, but it would be more absurd for you to miss out on what, for you, is the type of riding you live for. I will be fine. Beat it."

Not to belabor the point, I said, "Just to clarify, you are ordering me to go on?"

Wayne gave me a confused look.

I explained, "Lisa said that I can't leave you unless you order me — not tell me, not ask me, not suggest to me — to go on."

Wayne cracked up. "Ok buddy, I order you to go. Get the hell out of here."

With clean conscience, I thanked Wayne, wished him good luck, told him I would wait for him in Silver City, and got the hell out of there.

By then it was after 9:30PM and dark, so I flicked on both my headlamp and my handlebar light. I was deep into my 16th hour of riding on the day and laser focus was required to avoid making a false move and ending up splattered at the bottom of a ravine. I mystically connected with the rhythm and flow of the trail and the serenity of being alone on the top of a mountain ridge with my sole concern in life whittled down to the patch of ground illuminated directly in front of me. After 30 minutes of twisting and turning and swooping and leaning and balancing and dropping and intensely concentrating, it occurred to me that this solo venture through the dark was the quintessential denouement of my Tour Divide experience. Ironically and poetically, I also realized that this ride at that moment was directly analogous to the graduation ceremony performed on the final day of every First Descents' program.

The First Descents' graduation ceremony entails sending a participant either into the rapids, into the surf, or up the rock wall one final time without a guide and without others nearby. The purpose of the ritual is twofold. For one, it showcases and celebrates the participant's proficiency with a new sport. More significantly, it provides a solitary moment to reflect on everything they have overcome that week and, for many, how far they have come and grown since their cancer diagnoses.

My solo ride in the pitch-black dark atop that lonely ridge in southern New Mexico was my graduation ceremony on the Tour Divide. I spent the next hour reflecting on everything that I had been through over the last month, the hardships I endured, my terrification on the morning of June 8, the beauty and majesty I witnessed, the breaths taken away by awe, the friends made, the injuries sustained and yet managed or ignored, the emotional swings, the occasional boredom, the laughter, the tears, the sheer distance ridden on two rubber tires, the cancer survivors who will benefit from my ride and, ultimately, the legacy this adventure will leave for my daughters and, someday, their kids. It was an hour filled with deep introspective emotion combined with unbridled exhilaration resulting in an experience powerfully and indelibly etched in my memory.

My two-wheeled sashay across the final rooftop of the Gila Wilderness concluded with an invigorating and technical descent off the mountain and several rolling ups-and-downs on the paved road exiting the forest. As I passed a "Leaving Gila National Forest" sign, I felt competing emotions of elation and sadness . . . elation for the accomplishment, sadness that this incredible adventure was ending.

After a short punchy climb past a town called Pinos Altos, I buoyantly breezed down an intoxicating 7-mile pavement descent that rolled me into Silver City at 11:15PM. Like a moth darting toward light, I headed straight for a still-open McDonalds. While eating a feast fit for a King . . . and Queen . . . and their kids, I called the Comfort Inn across the street from McDonalds and booked a room. Still wired after eating, checking in and showering, I spent an hour constructing a blog on my iPhone summarizing the prior two days.

Every few minutes, I also checked Wayne's progress on the Trackleader's website and was relieved when he made it out of the Gila National Forest at 1:30AM. I assumed he would then come straight to the hotel with an arrival at around 2:30AM. I finished my blog at 2AM and noticed that Wayne's dot showed that he had stopped just past Pinos Altos. This was head scratching. When his dot had not moved by 2:15AM, I concluded that he stopped to take a nap at the base of the little climb out of Pinos Altos without realizing that a fast easy descent into Silver City awaited him just beyond the climb.

I turned off the lights and the phone with sweet satisfaction. The penultimate day of "Survivor - Tour Divide" was now behind me. We still had 125 miles to go to the finish, but they were supposedly "easy" miles with 20 miles of rolling pavement, 40 miles of dirt and then a 65-mile paved straight shot to Antelope Wells. Depending on our departure time in the morning, I targeted an arrival in Antelope Wells sometime between 8PM and midnight on Saturday night, July 7, well within the 30-day goal. I fell asleep contentedly imagining the finish at Antelope Wells and the huge hug I would give Lisa. Success on this journey would have been impossible without her love and support and I missed her dearly.

Morning in the Gila Valley

Gang of elk

At least one of us was regularly washing!

Rolling hills of the Gila

Start of the CDT

Night Riding on the CDT

Goodbye my friend

Chapter 43 - Well it's all right, riding around in the breeze
Well it's all right, if you live the life you please
Well it's all right, even if the sun don't shine
Well it's all right, we're going to the end of the line
— The Traveling Wilburys, *The End of the Line*

Tour Divide Day 30 - 127 miles - Silver City, NM to US/Mexico border at Antelope Wells, New Mexico. Bright light streaming through the curtains signaled the arrival of the final day of the Tour Divide. It was 6:45AM. I immediately grabbed my phone to check Wayne's whereabouts and found a text letting me know that he would be at the hotel by 7AM. Like clockwork, he walked in the door at 6:58AM. He confirmed that the short hill after Pinos Altos was the straw that broke his camel's back and he camped out on someone's front lawn. As I surmised, he had no idea that it was all descent to Silver City just over that hill.

We were wrecked from the last two days of strenuous and exhaustive riding, and minimal sleep. Therefore, we opted to spend our last morning chilling, eating a long breakfast at the hotel, and delaying departure until 9:30AM.

The route south from Silver City rolled up and down on the smooth and spacious shoulder of a highway. At mile 19, we turned off the pavement onto a hard-packed dirt road that took us 33 miles into the Chihuahuan Desert (with a missed turn that cost us two miles). Although it was a hot day, we covered the 51 (plus two) miles from Silver City in just under five hours, crossing under Interstate 10 and arriving at the Bowlin's Trading Post in Separ, NM at 2:30PM. I mention the Interstate as it was the last of the three major east-west coast-to-coast interstates that we crossed, the first being I-80 in Wyoming and the second being I-70 in Colorado.

The folks at Bowlin's love Tour Dividers and showed us instant hospitality by giving us seats, letting us start a food and drink tab, and asking us questions about where we were from, how we enjoyed the journey, why we did the ride, how we got the insanity gene, etc. During this time, we filled our now iron stomachs with Cokes, Gatorade, popsicles, potato chips, beef jerky and ice cream. Even though the end was so near, we were hot and spent and content to dawdle. We laughed at the crazy and garish souvenirs in the store and I suggested buying fireworks for the finish. Wayne intelligently remarked, "Uh Brent, considering the finish is an actual U.S. border crossing manned by federal agents, maybe shooting off fireworks would not be the smartest idea." True.

We rolled out of Bowlin's at 3:45PM after a prolonged 75 minutes of

247

lollygagging. The next eight miles were on a dirt road right next to I-10. This was the last dirt we would ride on the Tour. At 4:30PM, we passed the iconic "Antelope Wells - Hachita" exit sign and turned onto Route 146 which would take us due south for 65 miles on pavement, ending at Antelope Wells.

Just after making the turn onto Route 146, we pulled up next to a car parked on the side of the road just beyond the bottom of the exit ramp. Standing next to the car was a gorgeous brunette and her two dogs. I gave Lisa a warm hug and kiss, but sadly my dogs did not even recognize me. Lisa and the pups drove 11 hours from Avon, Colorado to escort us the rest of the way.

The first 18 miles of the paved road were hot, boring and slow. Why slow? Any guesses? If you have been reading these posts, what has been our constant nemesis since leaving Steamboat in Colorado? What are Headwinds for $1,000 Alex! I was too tired to care. It was what it was.

We reached the village of Hachita at 6PM and found an open convenience store where we lounged inside devouring popsicles and Cokes. The store was air-conditioned and contained a couple leather booths. We hung out for 30 minutes waiting for the sun to hide behind a bank of menacing clouds. Lisa was both amused and aghast by our gourmandization of those poor popsicles. 47 miles to go.

We left the convenience store as the skies darkened. Rain appeared imminent. At that point, I welcomed rain, snow or hail as all would provide relief from the blaring sun. While no precipitation fell, the clouds brought a pleasant drop in temperature. Additionally, the wind direction and road direction both changed just slightly enough that the wind became neutral and we covered the next 27 miles in just over two hours.

With each mile, Wayne and I reminisced about the highs and lows of the past month, and shared some laughs over so many of the things we had seen, done and experienced. It was a figurative ride down memory lane.

We took one more brief break at the 20-mile mark and used the break to finish our last Gatorade and turn on our lights. Then we simply pounded out the final miles, both pedaling side by side in rhythmic unison, counting down the miles one at a time as we passed green fluorescent mile-markers every three minutes or so. With ten miles to go, it was pitch dark except for distant lightning flashes, the light from my headlamp (Wayne's headlamp battery had just died), and the glow of Lisa's taillights in the distance.

Nine, eight, seven, six. Although, the last ten miles actually consisted of a 400-foot climb to the border, we sustained an 18mph pace. Excited much? With five miles to go, the yellow lights of Antelope Wells came into view.

Four, three, two.

The final road sign said "Antelope Wells Point of Entry 1 Mile." We were three minutes away. Emotion and excitement overcame me as I tried to envision the final moment of the ride. Would I cry? Would I laugh? Would I scream?

With a quarter-mile to go, we could see Lisa's car parked by a sign in front of a lit-up but otherwise deserted complex. We eased off the accelerators after an hour of manic pedaling and coasted the last few hundred yards, rolling to a stop next to Lisa. Wayne and I gave each other a monster hug. I gave Lisa a monster hug. Lisa gave Wayne a monster hug. I emitted a few primal whelps of joy and then looked at Wayne and said, "I'll race you back to Canada. Let's go!"

Lisa handed us some beers and we toasted, chugged, and posed for pictures. I donned a Washington Capitals hockey jersey for one photo and a Colgate University bike jersey for another. The scene was odd and anticlimactic and oddly anticlimactic. The border was closed and we were the only ones there. There were no congratulatory banners, medals or fanfare. There was just eerie silence broken only by the occasional sounds of distant barking dogs, and darkness interrupted only by intermittent bursts of lightning.

As for emotions, I did not cry, I did not laugh, I did not scream. To be honest, I was in an emotionless numb daze and heading down the path to catatonia. I think the breadth of the accomplishment was so overwhelming that my brain froze. All I knew was that it was time to stop riding my bike and go home. We slowly packed the car, threw our bikes on the rack and gave a final sentimental nod toward Mexico. We then got in the car, turned north for the first time in 30 days, and drove away.

The final dirt climb of the Tour Divide

My steed's final nap on the Tour Divide

Finished!

Iconic Antelope Wells Exit sign

We did it!

The final stats

EPILOGUE— "These are days you'll remember
Never before and never since, I promise
will the whole world be warm as this"
— 10,000 Maniacs, *These are Days*

Approximately 182 racers started from Banff on June 8, 2018. Wayne and I finished tied for 58th place. Only two more racers finished during the night and early morning hours of of July 7-8 to break the 30-day mark. Another handful finished in the days and weeks to follow. For those doing the math, that is a finish rate of well under 50%. My final mileage tally was 2,731 miles. My final cumulative elevation gain was 219,789 feet, which is the equivalent of climbing from sea level to the summit of Mt. Everest over seven times. My final weight was 145 pounds, 14 pounds less than my starting weight. As of this writing, I have gained it all back!

The Tour was won by a young guy named Lewis Ciddor on Day 16. Crazily, that did not break the Tour record. In interviews after the race, he said he slept an average of three hours per night. Insanity. My brief riding mates on Day 1, Gary Johnson and Jacki K, finished the Tour on Day 28. Ironically, they found each other halfway through the race and rode most of the last two weeks together. Chuck Lee reached Antelope Wells at 11AM on Sunday morning (day 31). Chuck insists that he tried to catch us after Pie Town, but we put 30 miles on him by the end of that day and it was too much ground to make up. Mario Hamel and Vincent Hamel were stuck in Plataro, Colorado for two days awaiting Vincent's bike part. They reached Antelope Wells on Monday evening (day 32).

Grace Ragland started the race with a horrific cold that worsened during her 100-mile first day. She spent two nights recovering in Elkford, British Columbia and that delay set her far back from the pack. She continued solo for a solid week before catching some other riders in Montana. Amazingly, despite multiple physical issues, many relating to her Multiple Sclerosis, Grace finished the Tour on Day 42. Heroic.

The whereabouts of Bro Dude and/or the Kid remain unknown.

In the days and weeks following the Tour, I was useless. Expectedly, I was physically sore, spent and drained. Surprisingly, the mental impact was more dramatic. My focus was nonexistent, my mind wandered constantly, I could not hold a lengthy conversation, and I was generally distant around other humans. Lisa said that she assumed that I would be a slug on the couch for several weeks, but had no idea that I would be such a stranger. I was also disinterested in most anything going on around me or in the world.

Prior to the race, I read voraciously and was somewhat addicted to politics and the news. After the race, I no longer cared about politics or news. Spending time in the wilderness changed my perspective. I realized and determined that day-to-day political dramas are unimportant and have so little impact on my life that the time spent paying attention to them is simply wasted time and energy. For two months following the Tour, I did not read the newspaper and the only television that I watched was sports and an occasional movie with Lisa. I also re-watched the *Ride the Divide* movie and was shocked by how easy the race looked on video. Definitely false advertising!

It is now late-November and the mid-term U.S. elections are over. I ignored the hoopla. It still just seemed like unhealthy noise and silly drama and I have not rediscovered a yen for noise or drama. Maybe I never will again and maybe that is a good thing. I thought of researching whether science could explain my mental state post-Tour. Upon reflection, I think it was simply a case of "brain-fry." As I mentioned at the end of Chapter 36, the amount of thinking and planning and calculating (and worrying) required to make it through a day on the Tour far exceeded the brainpower that I utilized in a normal day of life, even one at the office. Multiply that cerebral output by 30 consecutive days and it was no wonder that I shutdown starting Day 31.

Throughout the Tour, I wondered how soon I would ride a bike again after the race. Many veteran riders share that they did not look at their bikes for months after the Tour, much less ride them. I was the opposite. During the last week of the Tour, I could not wait to get home and ride my "normal" mountain bike. Although I was still physically broken, I did my first ride three days after the Tour and felt surprisingly good. Over the next few weeks, I suffered some lingering ill effects from the Tour such as numb fingers, sore wrists, sore glutes and achy lower back, but had a blast mounting a bike with no bags and was contented by the welcome promise of a long afternoon nap.

Five weeks after the Tour, I raced my 12th Leadville 100. I had no idea how my body would respond and figured my performance would fall somewhere between best-ever and disintegration. I felt strong the first couple hours of the race, but realized that I did not have the legs for "best ever" and just settled into a nice long day in the Colorado mountains. It was my most stress-free Leadville race in 12 years and I endeavored to smile and have fun throughout the day. I finished in a respectable 9 hours and 42 minutes and never once regretted participating so soon after the Tour.

Writing this book was actually easy as it allowed me to continue living the race and I attacked the book writing with the same intensity that I attacked the ride itself. After completing the final chapter, I asked myself the following six questions in an attempt to tie everything together: (1) What did I learn from the experience? (2) Did I change from the experience? (3) Would I do anything differently if I could go back in time? (4) Would I do the race again? (5) What is now on the bucket list? (6) What about the Tour Divide gives me the most pride? It may be months and even years before I have lucid answers to some of these questions, but I will take a stab for now.

(1) What did I learn from the experience?

I learned that I could be emotional and prone to tears. I learned that I could be both mentally and physically weak while still being mentally and physically tough as nails. I learned that we live in a huge vast country with lots and lots of cows. I learned that getting out in the wilderness is quite an antidote for all of the noise that pervades and invades our daily lives. I learned that being alone for prolonged periods is not as easy as it sounds and that I needed people more than I previously thought. I learned that playing in the mud could really suck. I learned that the human body is an amazing piece of machinery and is capable of far more than I ever imagined. I lost count of the number of times I went to sleep after a particularly hard day on the Tour wondering how I could possibly wake up and do it again. And yet, I woke up and did it again . . . and again . . . and again . . . and (you get the picture).

I learned that the Wind River Valley in Wyoming is one of the most breathtaking places on earth and is now the first place I visit in my mind when I try to escape the noises of life. I learned that as much as I love the outdoors and nature, I prefer a warm bed to a sleeping pad. I learned that the Tour Divide diet is an illusion as I have already re-gained all of the weight that I lost, plus a few pounds! I learned that life should not be limited or limiting. I learned that there could be beauty and fulfillment in misery. I learned that there are drag queens in Montana. I learned that there are crazy people who compete in Deca Ironman triathlons. Speaking of crazy people, I learned that on the spectrum of crazy people, there is a large disparity between moderately nutty people and uber batshit cuckoo people like Wayne, Mario, and anyone who completed the Tour Divide in under 20 days. Despite my occasional whining and bitching about weather and mud, I learned how to accept things, MANY things (including weather and mud), that I could not control. Finally, I learned that I love my wife and daughters more than I possibly knew beforehand.

(2) Did I change from the experience?

Lisa might disagree, but other than a shift in perspective, I do not feel that I changed as a person. As mentioned earlier, I did not find religion or spiritual purpose or have any sudden epiphanies about the direction of my life. I was not prone to 'sweating the small stuff' before the Tour and am less so now. Prior to the Tour, I was not overly concerned about what people thought of me. After the Tour, it matters less. To quote Popeye the Sailor Man, "I yam what I yam!" I have always been adventurous and willing to take a risk, but I think I am even more adventurous now. It will be interesting to see how the Tour experience opens the door for different adventures, not just for me, but for Lisa as well. The more applicable question might be whether I grew from the experience. I think the jury will be out on that question for quite a while.

(3) Would I do anything differently if I could go back in time?

This is a question I have revisited often since Antelope Wells. The competitive side of me is curious whether I had the strength and fortitude to be a 23-27 day finisher. Regardless, I would not materially change anything. Maybe just a series of little things. For one, I would not start the race with a two-liter plastic bottle attached to my front fork. I would get to Banff a couple days earlier to acclimate. I would overdose on electrolytes in Banff. I would not take three weeks off from riding before the race. I would have stuck with Gary Johnson longer as he would have been fun company. I would have gone with a bivy-sac over a tent. I would have run smaller width tires. I would have taken the left rut on Fleecer Ridge instead of the right rut. Actually, that is just stupid. I should have just walked down Fleecer Ridge. From a pure race-strategy standpoint, I would have left the Best Western in Fernie at 5AM instead of 11AM. However, I am glad I piddled that morning, as I would not have met my new BFF Wayne Kurtz.

(4) Would I do the race again?

This is an interesting question as I equate the Tour Divide experience with that of a woman giving birth. During the latter stages of pregnancy and during the delivery itself, a woman screams, "Never again!!" Then time passes, she has a beautiful baby girl or boy, and all of the painful memories are forgotten. My painful Tour memories have faded and the good ones have become more vivid and dominant. One of the reasons I wrote this book is to remind myself of the myriad crappy moments on the Tour so that I would not get any stupid ideas about doing it again. It's not working. I still think about the race daily. While there were many sections of tedium and a few sections of abject misery (Koko Claims, Bannack Road), I relished the adventure, freedom, simplicity and solitude. I also would love to see Montana in good weather. Long story short, I would do it again, but probably not anytime soon . . . particularly if I want to stay married.

(5) What is now on the bucket list?

The bucket list is currently empty. In less than 6 months, I crossed off the top three major items on my list, which were to see the Caps win a Stanley Cup, complete the Tour Divide, and write a book. I am sure the list will not stay blank for long. There are rides and races I would like to do, but my life will not be lacking if I do not do them. I would love to get Lisa into bikepacking so that we can share these types of adventures together. I do not ever see her becoming an avid mountain biker, so trips with her will likely be of the road-bikepacking variety with nightly hotel stays. One trip we are contemplating someday is a bike trip down the west coast from Vancouver to San Diego. I would also love to tour internationally with Lisa when the time is right. From a mountain-biking standpoint, I would love to bikepack the 500-mile Colorado Trail or large sections of the new Wild-West Trail that bisects Arizona, Utah and Idaho and parallels the Great Divide Route. There is also currently an off-road route under construction that will someday connect Canada to Mexico through Oregon, Washington and California. That will be pretty amazing. Finally, the competitive Brent would like to break 8 hours and 30 minutes in Leadville.

(6) What about the Tour Divide gives me the most pride?

I am incredibly proud of this achievement; so proud that I wrote a friggin' book about it! However, there is no single thing that gives me the most pride, so I will list a few.

First, I persevered after my Day 2 meltdown and after managing several injuries that threatened to end my race at various stages.

Second, I love that Wayne and I finished strong by covering 375 challenging miles in three days to finish in under 30 days. I am well aware that there are guys (and gals) who did this race a lot faster and who put in significantly more mileage per day and for whom 375 miles in three days is not a big deal. Well, based on our performance through the first 27 days and compared to most cyclists in the world who probably could not last a day on the Tour Divide, those three days were a big deal to us.

Third is not really a pride thing, but I thoroughly enjoyed sharing this adventure and interacting with my friends and family through Facebook. Unless all of said friends were blowing smoke up my ass with their comments and praise, I believe my daily updates provided both entertainment as well as a vicarious summer diversion for them.

Finally, the most important and obvious achievement is the incredible impact this ride will have on First Descents and the young adult cancer community. I have received many comments telling me how heroic I am for raising so much money through my Tour Divide fundraiser. However, I would like to inject some accuracy and perspective. I did not write a massive donation check. Instead, I shamelessly asked and hopefully inspired a community of friends and family to give. The money came from all of us. Everyone who wrote a check or clicked on the donation link and parted with some shekels shares a slice of heroism. For that, I cannot thank every donor enough. Together, we raised over $190,000 for FD (as of November 30, 2018), an amount that covered nearly half of all of First Descents' new programming in 2018. That is incredible and impactful and I will continue to try to find ways and avenues to reach my $200,000 goal (including donating any proceeds from the sale of this book) and then will gear up to start a new campaign in 2019. If you are reading this and want to donate, simply Google "Brent Goldstein First Descents Tour Divide" and click the first link that appears.

So that is my story and I am sticking to it. It was a massive and epic adventure generating memories that I will cherish and stories that I will spin for the rest of my life. If you have read this far, thank you for letting me share my journey. I hope my story will inspire you to get outside and seek your own challenge or go out and simply explore. Do not say "I can't." Believe me, you can. Everybody can. Special athletic talent or ability are not prerequisites to engage in a meaningful challenge. I certainly do not possess any special athletic qualities. A little blend of discipline, desire and commitment are all that is needed to tackle a challenge and succeed. Give me a few days' notice, and I may even join you! CARPE DIEM

ACKNOWLEDGEMENTS:

Thanks to my buddies Gary Morris and Kevin Kane, who were always by their phones and/or computers to text me information (via my iPhone and my Garmin inReach) about upcoming distances, elevation changes or weather changes and were always quick to provide encouragement. Thanks boys. I also got daily texts of encouragement from my old friend Jeff Hoffman and from my riding buddies Larry Etman, Brian Peyser, Kenny Lipsman, Ed Wallach and David Flyer and countless similar periodic texts and messages from various friends and family that carried me through some low times. I will remember all of them.

To the Bernstein sisters (Lisa and Amy), you both were amazing in sharing my story on Facebook at every turn. Special similar thanks to Eric Fretz, Melissa Rebecca Madden, Andrea Obbie Kay, Joe Laycock, Michael Wilson, Jolie Deutschman, Mark Raker, Stephen Rodgers, Matt Delaney, Brent Cantor, Daryn Goldstein, Lindsay Forbes, April Capil and Alyson Achorn for sharing the story and donation link on their Facebook pages.

To Brian at the Bike Doctor bike shop in Frederick, all of your advice, fixes and fittings were spot-on. Thank you for turning my Salsa Timberjack into the perfect Tour Divide machine and for turning me into a mediocre mechanic (which was a huge step-up).

To Mario Hamel, Vincent Hamel and Wayne Kurtz, thanks for adopting me on Day 3. I loved riding with you and getting to know you all and hope that our paths cross on new adventures in the future. To Chuck Lee, I am so glad you joined us in Lima. You are an awesome guy and, at 68 years old, a TOTAL STUD AND INSPIRATION. I can only hope that I am still doing this stuff when I am 68.

To every single one of you who supported my First Descents' Tour Divide fundraiser, THANK YOU THANK YOU THANK YOU. A difference was made for people who need it.

To John "Wobber" Wontrobski, thanks for making the trip and providing us with essential groceries at the Colorado-New Mexico border. You are a Trail Angel Brother!

To Lisa Goldstein, Arlyn Goldstein, Kim and Larry Weinberg, Kelly Malin, Laurel McHargue, Nancy Samit, Wayne Kurtz, Chuck Lee, John Wontrobski and Lynn Schwartz, thanks for proofreading, editing and feedback. I never understood the value of proofreading and editing until going through this process.

To Devin Schain, thanks for the invaluable strategic marketing and distribution advice.

To Neil Cohen, Julian Marsh, Max Greco and everyone else at District Photo in Beltsville, Maryland, thanks for helping me get this story formatted and printed for distribution.

To Bonnie Gagnon, thanks for answering a million questions and opening the door.

To Grace Ragland, thanks for sharing your rookie pre-race journey with me and for inspiring the hell out of me along the way (and congrats for your own accomplishment!).

To Jacki K, thanks for saving my ass on Day 2.

To Chuck Ludden, thanks for the medication in Whitefish.

To the thousands of cows along and on the roads, thanks for the company and sounds.

To everyone at First Descents, thanks for being so supportive and so awesome and for doing everything you do every day for young adults coping with cancer.

To my parents, siblings and kids, I hope I have made you all proud and set an example. And thanks Mom for the Bic lighter!

To Allan Goldberg, thanks for changing my life with a single phone-call. I miss you every day. In a way, this ride was for you.

To Lisa, I love you so much. You are truly my everything and I wouldn't have even made it on the plane to Canada without you. (Though I guess I could have taken an Uber to the airport). ☺)

APPENDIX A
GEAR LIST

BIKE

Salsa Timberjack 27.5+ w/1X12 Eagle Drivetrain
Schmidt Son Dynamo hub for front wheel
Cane Creek Thudbuster Seat Post
Jones H-Bar handlebar
Profile Design T2+ DL Clip-on Aerobars
Salsa Anything Cages with Straps (2)
Saddle- Brooks B17 Imperial Saddle
Time Atac XC8 Carbon Pedals

SLEEP

Tent: Big Agnes Fly Creek UV1 w/MtnGlo
Tent Footprint - Big Agnes
Sleeping Pad: REI Co-op Flash Insulated 25X72
Enlightened Equipment Revelation Quilt
Sea to Summit Thermolite Reactor Extreme Liner
Dry Bags - Sea to Summit Dry Bags

CLOTHES

Patagonia Ultralite Down Jacket - Medium
Outdoor Research Helium II Rain Jacket
Marmot PreCip Full-Zip Rain Pants - Men's Short
Revelcloud Insulated Vest
Merino Base Layer Wool T-Shirt
Merino Base Layer Wool long-sleeve shirt
Arm warmers and leg warmers
Thin arm warmers
First Descents bike kit (shorts and jersey)

Wool socks (2 pairs)
Waterproof socks
Long fingered gloves
Waterproof light mitten covers
Headbands and wool hat
Xero Z-Trail foldable sandals
Pearl Izumi X-Alp Bike shoes
T-shirt
running shorts
long underwear bottoms

ELECTRONICS
Garmin E-Trex 30 Bike computer
Garmin Edge 800 bike computer
Garmin - Inreach Satetllite Tracking Device
Sinewave Recharghable Cache
kLite Bikepacker Pro Dynamo Light and Switch
Anker 13000 mAh PowerCore rechargeable battery
Petzl Actik Core Headlamp
GoPro Hero4 Camera
iPhone 6
JBL Bluetooth Speaker
Various cords and two-output charger

BIKE BAGS
Revelate Designs Sweetroll Handlebar Bag
Revelate Designs Terrapin Saddle Bag
Rogue Panda Designs 3-compartment frame bag
Revelate Designs Mountain Feebag Handlebar Bags (2)
Revelate Designs Jerrycan Tube/Seatpost bag
Revelate DesignsMag Tank Top Tube Bag

B

MISCELLANEOUS
OTTO Lock 30" Bike Lock
Whistle
Loksak Opsak Odor Free Bags (X2)
Mosquito Head Netting
Counter Assault Bear Deterrent Spray - 8.1 fl. oz.
Aquamira Water Purifying Drops
MSR DromLite Bag - 4 Liters
Exped Inflatable Pillow
Osprey Talon 11 Pack plus Osprey 2-litre Hydraulics Reservoir
Medical kit
AA Batteries
Rear Flashing Tail-light
Bike repair tools and kit (tubes, patches, spokes, tape, multi-tool, etc.)
Swiss Army Knife

APPENDIX B
ABOUT THE AUTHOR AND COHORTS

*Jackson Lake and the Tetons
(Chuck, Brent, Wayne, Mario, Vincent).
My Favorite Picture of the Tour Divide*

Brent Goldstein. Brent was born, raised and continues to make his home in the Maryland suburbs of Washington D.C.. Brent graduated with Bachelor of Arts degree from Colgate University in 1989 and a Juris Doctor degree from Georgetown University Law Center in 1993. Brent spent 6+ years in private law practice in the late 90s where he specialized in corporate, general business, private securities and real estate law. In late 1999, he took a position as a Vice President-Senior Counsel for the healthcare finance division of Heller Financial and, following GE Capital's acquisition of Heller Financial in 2001, Brent switched from the legal side to the business side and spent two years with GE in loan underwriting and risk management.

Growing tired of corporate bureaucracy, Brent left GE Capital in 2003 to join his father, Mark, and formed a new business called Avanti Capital that specialized in sourcing, structuring and raising capital for real estate transactions and "one-off" non-real estate green-technology venture capital transactions. Simultaneously, Brent also formed Goldstein Legal PC to handle the legal work for the various Avanti Capital transactions as well as to perform contract transactional work for clients.

In addition to his business pursuits, Brent has been very active in philanthropic endeavors. He served on the National Board of Directors of Maccabi USA from 2000 to 2003 and was Chairman of the Washington D.C. Maccabi USA annual golf fundraiser from 1994 to 2013. Brent also served as Vice President of the Washington D.C. Chapter of American ORT from 2004 to 2007, a Member of the Board of Directors of the Washington D.C. Chapter of American ORT from 2002 to 2009 and Chairman of the Washington D.C. American ORT annual golf fundraiser from 1999 through 2012. He has served on event committees for Capital Camps, Hebrew Home of Greater Washington, and the U.S. Olympic Committee. Finally, Brent is currently the Chairman of the Board of Directors for the First Descents cancer organization (www.firstdescents.org), a national organization that provides outdoor adventure programs for young-adult (ages 18-40) cancer survivors and fighters. Since 2007, Brent has spearheaded a fundraising campaign that has raised over $1.5Million for First Descents through his annual participation as a competitor in the ultra-endurance Leadville 100 mountain bike race held every August in Leadville, Colorado.

Brent lives in Rockville, Maryland with Lisa, his wife since 1992. Together they have three daughters – Daryn (born in 1995), Arlyn (born in 1999) and Bailey (born in 2001), and three dogs – Dexter, Simba and Cody. His recreational interests are skiing, golf, biking (mountain and road), ice hockey, hiking and spending as much time each year in the mountains of Colorado as is reasonably and professionally possible

<u>Wayne Kurtz</u>. Wayne was born and raised in Pittsburgh, Pennsylvania and still calls it home. His background is finance and accounting, but he has spent his professional career doing a variety of things from working for a big six accounting firm, a national consulting firm, a Fortune 500 company, his own companies (he launched several), and an insurance company. He is a Type-A goal-setter and always strives to reach for new heights with his goals, whether in business or athletics. He shared with me that "if your friends and family don't say the words 'no way, you're crazy' about your

goals then you have not made them big enough!"

Wayne is a die-hard fan of all Pittsburgh sports teams and particularly lives, eats, breathes and dies for the Steelers. Wayne was a competitive swimmer and baseball player growing up, but discovered triathlon in his late teens. Triathlons not only became his passion, but they soon became the "building block to everything else" in his life. He began with Olympic distance triathlons in his 20s, but that wasn't enough so he worked his way up to the Ironman distance. That wasn't enough so he started competing in "Deca Ironman" competitions. A "Deca" Ironman works in one of two ways. In one, you do an Ironman a day for 10 consecutive days. In the other, you compete in one mega long triathlon that is 10X the normal Ironman distance (i.e., 24-mile swim, 1,120 mile bike and 260-mile run). But even that wasn't enough for Wayne, so he somehow found a bunch of like-minded insane people and competed in a "TRIPLE-DECA IRONMAN" where one completes a full Ironman a day for 30 consecutive days!

Wayne still competes around the world and has raced for 32 years and participated in several hundred endurance races including: triathlon, running, cycling, snowshoe, adventure, and swimming races. Wayne's friends call him "Wayne The Train" and the "Grinder" as he pushes to always finish no matter how bad the circumstances. He has coached a small group of athletes for 21 years and writes though his popular blogs on endurance sports training, entrepreneurism and chief goals officer platform on http://blog.wayne-kurtz.com. Wayne has written several books about his competitions and the life lessons he has learned along the way, including "*Beyond The Iron*" and "*Never Say 'I Wish I Had*'", and has co-authored "*Stronger Than Iron*" (the epic world record journey of the athletes who finished the 2013 Triple DECA Iron event) and his most recent book "*It's All About the DECA*."

In 2016, Wayne competed in his first self-supported bikepacking event, the 4,400+ mile TransAmerica bike race from the Oregon Coast to the Virginia Coast and decided that he loved ultra-long endurance events (i.e., 30 days or more) and did not want to wait another three years after TransAmerica to do another one. So in January of 2018 he targeted the Tour Divide as his next big challenge, despite being primarily a road-biker.

Wayne is married to his "Greek Queen" Jan and says that he is blessed that she is not only his best friend and his biggest supporter, but also his greatest influence. Most of all, he is thankful that Jan is willing to let Wayne be Wayne each time he chooses his next crazy adventure. Jan and Wayne have no kids, but they have "a million" god-children and love spoiling them all.

Mario Hamel. Mario is from Montreal, Canada. He earned a Bachelor of Engineering from the Royal Military College of Canada in 1989 and spent the early 90s as a flight instructor, fighter pilot and maintenance test pilot for the Royal Canadian Air Force. He left the RCAF in about 1996 and held various positions including Ops Manager, Program Manager, and Vice-President with the Northern Lights Aerobatic Team.

In 2007, Mario became an entrepreneur and has spent the last 11 years investing in real estate, building up a real estate management company and overseeing several small business ventures. During this time, he has also continued flying planes, mostly in aerobatic airshows.

About 6 years ago, Mario discovered triathlon and, like Wayne, moved with ease from Olympic distance, to half-Ironman to full Ironman before realizing that he wanted more. So two years ago, he discovered the world of ultra-Ironman and began devoting his training to long distances. Forged with incredible discipline from his years in the RCAF and blessed with amazing strength and stamina, Mario's jump to ultra-triathlon was a major success as he achieved a 3rd place ranking with the International Ultra Triathlon Association.

Spending countless hours on a bike saddle was nothing new for Mario, but doing it in a fully unsupported endurance race across mountain ranges on a mountain bike was a new world for him.

Mario has been married to his wife Micheline for over 30 years and has two adult children, Marie and Vincent.

Vincent Hamel. Mario's son Vincent was 24 years old at race-start and has spent most of his life in Montreal, Canada. Vincent grew up as an avid skier and, at 15 years old, he declared to his parents that his dream was to move out west and be a ski bum. So he finished high school and at 19, moved to Banff, Alberta, Canada to spend two years living his dream. During his time in Banff, he worked as a ski instructor while also becoming an expert backcountry skier.

Although Vincent had developed a deep passion for the outdoors while living in Banff, he realized that making a living as a ski-bum would be a challenge. With pragmatism trumping passion, Vincent returned to Montreal at age 21 to attend University and spent from 2014 through 2017 earning his Bachelors Degree in Psychology. He is currently studying for a Masters degree in Human Resources Management.

During his first year at University, Vincent took a part-time winter job at a ski-shop near his campus. When winter ended, the ski shop converted to a bike shop and Vincent remained as an employee and developed a new passion for biking. The bike shop where Vincent works is one of the few bike shops in Quebec that specializes in and supports bikepacking and Vincent soon learned about the Tour Divide. Although he was new to mountain biking, it sounded like something he would love to do. So he told Mario about it and the rest is history.

<u>Chuck Lee</u>. Chuck was born in 1949 in Portsmouth, Virginia, which made him 68 years young when he started the Tour Divide. Chuck grew up in a Navy family and spent his youth in Chicago, Illinois and San Diego, California before settling in 1961 in New Bern, North Carolina when his Dad retired. Chuck attended North Carolina State University in Raleigh and majored in Engineering Operations (manufacturing engineering and production control).

After college, Chuck joined the Navy Aviation Officer Candidate program in Pensacola, Florida (the movie 'An Officer and A Gentleman' was loosely based on this program). It was there that Chuck got his first 10-speed and began a love-affair with bikes. After finishing the Aviation program, Chuck moved up to Oceania Naval Air Station in Virginia Beach to train as a bombardier/ navigator in the A6 Intruder, a medium sized, carrier-based, all weather bomber. He worked the ground mapping radar, bomb switches, navigation, etc. and also spent two stints "cruising" aboard the USS Saratoga, followed by some time at duty station in Puerto Rico and then a two-year assignment with the USS Enterprise near Seattle, Washington in 1980.

Before starting with the Enterprise, Chuck was given 30 days leave plus travel time. In Chuck's words: "I thought 'heck, I bet I can ride a bike across the country in 30 days.' He picked a bike out of a catalog, got a better seat, real bike shoes and a decent pump, put it together and took off. He had no helmet, no lights, no gps and no phone and his clothes were just basic cotton. He arrived in San Jose, California in 28 days and says "it was a great trip!"

After leaving the Navy in 1984, Chuck flew over to England and bought a boat, a 33 foot sloop, and sailed down to Portugal for the winter and cruised the Mediterranean the next summer before turning west and sailing it across the Atlantic to and through the Windward and Leeward Islands, BVI, USVI, Puerto Rico and the Bahamas on the way back home to North Carolina.

He continued to do a lot of sailing, delivery work, charter-captain work and racing when he met his future wife Leslie at a regatta in 1989 and said something smooth like "why don't you quit your job and sail to New Zealand with me?!" She did! They left North Carolina in January, 1990 and circumnavigated the globe via the Caribbean Islands, Venezuela, Colombia, Panama, French Polynesia, Samoa, Tonaga, New Zealand, Australia, South Africa and back home thru the Caribbean and Bahamas, returning in July, 1994, after four and a half years. Chuck joked that his land friends said "what took so long?" and his sailing friends said 'what was the rush?"

After his global trip was over, Chuck picked up where he left off with sailing, racing
and delivering boats up and down the east coast and to the Caribbean while Leslie worked in a nautical retail store. Sometime around 2000, Chuck began working for the local YMCA camps near here New Bern and at Camps Sea Gull and Seafarer as Captain of their 60' power catamaran. In 2008, he took a summer off and spent five months hiking the Application Trail from Georgia to Maine.

Chuck first heard about the first Trans America bike race in 2014, saw the movie '*Inspired To Ride*,' and started dreaming about riding across the country again. He retired from the camp job after the 2015 season and headed to Astoria, Oregon in the summer of 2016 to start the TransAm race. That's where Chuck first met Wayne. Chuck enjoyed TransAmerica (did it in under 30 days), but felt he could have done better.

In the winter of 2017, Chuck's buddy Jeremiah presented Chuck with the Tour Divide as a great new challenge. They had hoped to do it in the summer of 2017, but Jeremiah injured his shoulder and they put it off to 2018. At first they were just going to ride the Great Divide route at a time of their own choosing. But then Chuck learned that Wayne was going to race the Tour Divide and was able to convince Jeremiah to join him at the Grand Depart on June 8.

Chuck and Jeremiah started the 2018 Tour Divide together, but Jeremiah had physical issues from the get-go and cut his Tour short in Whitefish. Between his age and his lack of mountain bike experience, Chuck wasn't keen about riding the rest of the Tour solo, so the chase was on to catch up to Wayne and he finally caught us in Lima, Montana.

J

www.ingramcontent.com/pod-product-compliance
Lightning Source LLC
Chambersburg PA
CBHW050627300426
44112CB00012B/1689